2017
BRITISH
WARSH
& AUXILIARIES

HMS Scimitar

THE ROYAL NAVY

Over the twelve months that have elapsed since the previous edition it may have appeared that the years of cuts and underfunding, suffered by the Royal Navy might be coming to an end. The first of the new carriers, QUEEN ELIZABETH, is scheduled to start sea trials in 2017. The Successor submarine programme has become the Dreadnought class as steel has been cut on the first of four new Trident missile carrying submarines. The Type 26 frigate programme is to begin production in the summer of 2017. A programme for a new class of general purpose frigate has been announced and procurement of five new Offshore Patrol Vessels is underway. It would seem, on paper, that the future of the RN is, at long last, looking positive. However, there are still too many capability gaps - just at the end of 2016 it was announced that the RN is to lose its anti-ship missile capability in 2018 as Harpoon is withdrawn without replacement. As a weapon it is out of date but the decision emphasises the need for long term planning, its replacement should have been in development 10 years ago and ready now to take over.   Manpower issues remain, particularly with engineers and submariners. Perhaps of most concern is the question of how the government will deliver the ambitious equipment procurement programme and whether there is sufficient funding and industrial capacity to resource this programme.

With the aircraft carrier programme well underway attention is now turning to the escort fleet and the need to replace the elderly Type 23 frigates. It is in this area that the RN has suffered the most over recent years. The 1998 SDSR determined that a minimum of 32 frigates and destroyers was, just, sufficient to meet operational commitments, although, even then senior officers expressed disquiet about the Navy's ability to cover directed tasks. Since then the number of escorts has been cut to just 19 ships. Of these the six Type 45 destroyers have machinery issues which are going to have to see new diesels fitted - a timetable for which has yet to be determined. The remaining thirteen ships are the Type 23 frigates which will start to decommission, one a year, from 2023. The standard operating tempo for deployments requires three ships for each commitment (one on station; one in transit and one in maintenance/work up) - allowing for ships in refit and two currently laid up in secondary roles alongside, the number of hulls available of the fleet planners is, to quote the Commons Defence Select Committee report of Nov '16, "woefully inadequate".

It was initially proposed that the thirteen Type 23 frigates would be replaced, on a one for one basis, by the new generation Type 26 frigates, or Global Combat Ships. The

SDSR 2015 reviewed the requirement for future escorts and determined that eight Type 26 would be configured for anti-submarine warfare, to replace the eight ASW capable Type 23s. The balance would be made up of a new general purpose frigate, the Type 31, which would be less costly and less complex than the Type 26. A minimum of five would be procured, and perhaps more; a potential increase in frigate numbers by 2035. All very encouraging, but government has not guaranteed funding nor set in place a firm programme. Governments change, priorities change and defence does not carry the same political clout as Health, Education or Welfare.

However, if MoD is able to fund this ambitious programme there needs to be a robust shipbuilding infrastructure in place to ensure delivery to what is now a very tight timetable.

At present UK complex warship construction is carried out by BAE Systems on the Clyde. In reality, BAE are the only remaining facility in the UK capable of undertaking such work. Famous names such as Vosper Thornycroft, Swan Hunter, Cammell Laird and Harland and Wolff, have all long since vanished from the shipbuilding landscape. With a single source of procurement, the MoD have, for many years, paid above market price for their warships to be built in the UK. Facilities on the Clyde, at Scotstoun and Govan, are dated and part of the Type 26 programme was to see a 'frigate factory' established on the Clyde which would introduce modern construction methods and allow production to become more competitive. In turn it was hoped that this could present export opportunities for UK built complex warships. The Type 26 could have good export potential with several nations looking to replace their frigate fleets in a similar timescale to the RN. However, the last UK built complex warships for export were the two Type 42 destroyers for Argentina and the Vosper Mk10 frigates for Brazil – and that was way back in the 1970s. The lack of investment in shipbuilding infrastructure has limited export potential and therefore all RN acquisitions have been bespoke, short production run designs - with a price tag to match. The reduction of the Type 26 programme from thirteen hulls to just eight makes the 'frigate factory' option unlikely. France, Italy, Spain, Germany and the Netherlands all have a modern warship building industry with strong records of exports while UK steadfastly fails to attract overseas sales. If Europe has so many good warship builders, why are complex warships not put out to international tender?

The government contends that the building of complex warships is a sovereign capability which must be maintained; to that end it is due to announce a National Shipbuilding Strategy (NSS) which should set out the framework under which the Type 26 and Type 31 frigates are to be delivered and ensure that the UK retains the workforce with the necessary skill sets and the facilities to produce such vessels. In the past such strategies have determined a drumbeat of work to retain a skilled workforce whilst guaranteeing a set amount of work under a Terms of Business Agreement (TOBA) should that drumbeat falter. It is to be hoped that any new NSS would address not only the modernisation of the shipbuilding facilities to improve and streamline production but also the introduction of competition to reduce prices. The NSS must also look at the wider UK industrial base because a true sovereign capability can only be such if the UK can provide the raw materials and support systems. Is it a sovereign capability if we have to source our specialist steel from France or Sweden or our weapons systems in collaboration with other European partners?

So, to build the Type 26 the MoD must get value for money and meet a timetable which will allow their introduction into the fleet without further reducing the current woefully small numbers of frontline escorts. The Type 26 manufacturing phase is already behind schedule as negotiations continue. BAE say that the design is still to be finalised while the MoD states they are not prepared to sign a contract until convinced they are getting the best value for money. Many suggest that the delays are due to a lack of funding - Lord West, a former First Sea Lord, has suggested that the RN is underfunded by some £750 million. In November 2016 the Secretary of State for Defence announced, in Govan, that the Type 26 would begin construction in the summer of 2017. However, it would seem that this was to demonstrate that the programme was moving forward rather than a firm commitment to construction; the caveat was "subject to final contract negotiations". The negotiations that have delayed the start of the build programme continue and therefore a summer 2017 start date cannot yet be guaranteed.

The Type 26 schedule remains tight and, if escort numbers are not to fall, is absolutely linked to the out of service dates of the Type 23 frigates. It has been reinforced over many years that there is no possibility of moving the Type 23 decommissioning dates; as such the first Type 26 must enter service in 2023 to relieve ARGYLL. Given a probable five-year build, Type 26 Hull-1 must start build this year. The new frigates are going to enter service with many of the sensors and weapons transferred from the older Type 23s. The first ship will have newly acquired systems to allow her to complete before ARGYLL leaves service - her equipment will then be transferred to Type 26 Hull-2 and so on. All seems logical except that the four non- ASW Type 23s are among the first five to decommission, so either the early Type 26s will enter service without the Type 2087 sonar, or it will be stripped off the later Type 23s before they leave service. Also, government have stated a drumbeat of 18-24 months for the Type 26 programme. If this is not addressed by NSS, the Type 23 frigates will be taken out of service faster than Type 26s are introduced. To achieve a one-for-one replacement the Type 26s must be built to a drumbeat of one per year, with Hull-8 replacing RICHMOND in 2030.

If the MoD do achieve the Type 26 programme, there still remains the follow-on Type 31. The first of these, theoretically lighter and cheaper, frigates will be required to replace SOMERSET in 2031. Assuming, once more, a five year build per ship, the Type 31 Hull-1 needs to be laid down in 2025. Given that the ship design is, as yet, undefined (the RN need a small crew; the MoD a cheap frigate and industry a lengthy period of work), urgency is essential. It is likely that BAE will be the prime contractor once again, but the Secretary of State for Defence Secretary during his announcement at Govan only said that the Clyde is in "pole position' for the contract which may leave the door open for an off the shelf purchase of a commercial design, similar to the Type 21 Amazon class.

What is increasingly obvious is that the SDSR 2015 aspirations are going to be very difficult to translate into physical assets without robust programme management and committed funding. The ambitious Type 26/31 shipbuilding programme is running in parallel to the acquisition of the Dreadnought class Trident missile submarine, which will devour a large chunk of the RN budget; the Astute class submarines and the need to refit the whole of the Type 45 class destroyers. The MoD must meet a very strict timeline to prevent the "woeful" number of escorts available to the RN becoming even fewer.

The UK has the 2nd largest budget in NATO, the largest in the EU, and the fifth largest in the world. It is one of only five countries to meet the NATO guideline to spend 2% of GDP on Defence. Surely this fact should enable UK to deliver better and more? As an island nation we will always need a strong Royal Navy and enough warships to keep our sea lanes of communications safe. If UK shipbuilding is unable to modernise and produce ships at a reasonable cost, perhaps it is time to start looking elsewhere for our much needed warships.

Steve Bush
Plymouth, November 2016

SHIPS OF THE ROYAL NAVY
Pennant Numbers

Ship	P. No.	Page	Ship	P. No.	Page
Aircraft Carriers			**Submarines**		
QUEEN ELIZABETH	R08	12	VANGUARD	S28	8
PRINCE OF WALES	*R09*	*12*	VICTORIOUS	S29	8
			VIGILANT	S30	8
Assault Ships			VENGEANCE	S31	8
			TORBAY	S90	11
OCEAN	L12	14	TRENCHANT	S91	11
ALBION	L14	15	TALENT	S92	11
BULWARK	L15	15	TRIUMPH	S93	11
			ASTUTE	S94	9
Destroyers			ARTFUL	S95	9
			AMBUSH	S96	9
DARING	D32	16	*AUDACIOUS*	*S97*	*9*
DAUNTLESS	D33	16	*ANSON*	*S98*	*9*
DIAMOND	D34	16	*AGAMEMNON*	*S99*	*9*
DRAGON	D35	16	*AJAX*	*S100*	*9*
DEFENDER	D36	16			
DUNCAN	D37	16	**Minehunters**		
Frigates			LEDBURY	M30	20
			CATTISTOCK	M31	20
KENT	F78	18	BROCKLESBY	M33	20
PORTLAND	F79	18	MIDDLETON	M34	20
SUTHERLAND	F81	18	CHIDDINGFOLD	M37	20
SOMERSET	F82	18	ATHERSTONE	M38	20
ST ALBANS	F83	18	HURWORTH	M39	20
LANCASTER	F229	18	QUORN	M41	20
ARGYLL	F231	18	PENZANCE	M106	22
IRON DUKE	F234	18	PEMBROKE	M107	22
MONMOUTH	F235	18	GRIMSBY	M108	22
MONTROSE	F236	18	BANGOR	M109	22
WESTMINSTER	F237	18	RAMSEY	M110	22
NORTHUMBERLAND	F238	18	BLYTH	M111	22
RICHMOND	F239	18	SHOREHAM	M112	22

Entries displayed in lighter typeface have yet to be completed

SUBMARINES
VANGUARD CLASS

Ship	Pennant Number	Completion Date	Builder
VANGUARD	S28	1992	VSEL
VICTORIOUS	S29	1994	VSEL
VIGILANT	S30	1997	VSEL
VENGEANCE	S31	1999	VSEL

Displacement 15,980 tons (dived) **Dimensions** 149.9m x 12.8m x 12m **Machinery** RR PWR2; 2 GEC Turbines, 27,000 hp; single shaft; pump jet propulsor; two auxiliary retractable propulsion motors **Speed** 25 + dived **Armament** 16 Tubes for Trident 2 (D5) missiles, 4 Torpedo Tubes **Complement** 135

Notes

After the successful UK D5 missile firing in May '94 the first operational patrol was carried out in early '95 and a patrol has been maintained constantly ever since. The UK's Trident missiles have been de-targeted since 1994, and the submarine on deterrent patrol is normally at several days notice to fire her missiles. The service life of the Vanguard class has been extended to beyond 2028 while at the same time reducing the number of operational missiles on each submarine to just eight. To achieve this five year extension three additional Long Overhaul Periods (LOPs) will be required, at Devonport, costing around £1.3 billion between 2014 and 2024. VANGUARD re-entered the refit cycle at the end of 2015.

HMS Ambush

ASTUTE CLASS

Ship	Pennant Number	Completion Date	Builder
ASTUTE	S94	2009	BAe Submarine Solutions
AMBUSH	S96	2012	BAe Submarine Solutions
ARTFUL	S95	2015	BAe Submarine Solutions
AUDACIOUS	*S97*	*2018*	*BAe Submarine Solutions*
ANSON	*S98*	*2020*	*BAe Submarine Solutions*
AGAMEMNON	*S99*	*2022*	*BAe Submarine Solutions*
AJAX	*S100*	*2024*	*BAe Submarine Solutions*

Displacement 7,400 tonnes (7,800 dived) Dimensions 97m x 11.2m x 9.5m Machinery RR PWR2; 2 Alsthom Turbines, 27,500 hp; single shaft; pump jet propulsor; two motors for emergency drive; one auxiliary retractable propellor Speed 29+ dived Armament 6 Torpedo Tubes; Spearfish torpedoes; Tomahawk cruise missiles for a payload of 38 weapons Complement 98 (Accommodation for 12 Officers and 97 Ratings)

Notes

Ordered in 1997, the Astute class will replace the Trafalgar class in RN service. In February 2016 ARTFUL, test fired her first torpedo using the BAE Systems designed Common Combat System (CCS), which functions as the digital 'brain' of the boat controlling its 'eyes', 'ears' and 'nervous system'. Using the torpedo test, the system was able to interpret sonar readings, and then attack a moving target with a practice weapon. The CCS, completed ahead of time so it was ready for the third rather than fourth Astute submarine, uses the latest technology to collect and process huge amounts of data from sensors such as sonar, providing key information to help inform important Command decisions.

All major fabrications for ANSON are now complete and awaiting assembly. The keel ring for the sixth submarine, AGAMEMNON, was ceremonially laid down on 18 July 2013. The seventh submarine, AJAX*, has been confirmed, but not yet ordered. In November 2015 the MoD awarded a contract for the delivery of ANSON, taking the total value for work on the vessel to £1.3 billion. The full contract covers the design and remaining build, test and commissioning activities on ANSON. Manufacturing commenced in 2010 and is on schedule to leave for sea trials in 2020.

The planned in-service dates for the remainder of the Astute class boats are: AUDACIOUS (2018); ANSON (2020); AGAMEMNON (2022) and AJAX (2024).

The Astute class is designed to fulfil a range of key strategic and tactical roles including anti-ship and anti-submarine operations, surveillance and intelligence gathering and support for land forces. Each boat will have a lock in lock out capability, enabling swimmers to leave the submarine while dived. This capability is in addition to the Chalfont dry deck hangar which can be fitted to the aft casing and designed to hold a swimmer delivery vehicle for stand off insertion.

*There is some confusion as to whether or not the seventh boat will be named AJAX. The name has been associated with the Astute class for some years and has appeared both in print and on the RN website, but this has now been removed. Whether or not the name was released unofficially or has fallen out of favour is unknown, but at present neither the MoD nor BAE refer to the vessel as anything other than Hull 7.

HMS Astute with Chalfont Dry Deck shelter. The aft section of conning tower fairing is removed to allow embarkation of the shelter. (Daniel Ferro)

HMS Torbay

TRAFALGAR CLASS

Ship	Pennant Number	Completion Date	Builder
TORBAY	S90	1986	Vickers
TRENCHANT	S91	1989	Vickers
TALENT	S92	1990	Vickers
TRIUMPH	S93	1991	Vickers

Displacement 4,500 tons 5,200 tons dived Dimensions 85.4m x 9.8m x 9.5m Machinery RR PWR1; 2 GEC Turbines, 15,000 hp; single shaft; pump jet propulsor; one motor for emergency drive - retractable propellor Speed 30+ dived Armament 5 Torpedo Tubes; Spearfish torpedoes; Tomahawk cruise missiles for a payload of 24 weapons Complement 130

Notes

All have undergone upgrades and received Type 2076 Sonar. Beginning in 2014 the submarines began a communications package upgrade to overcome obsolescence issues. With delays to the Astute class, decommissioning dates for the remaining T class have been extended. In August 2016 TRIUMPH returned to frontline operations following a maintenance period while TRENCHANT completed an extensive maintenance period at Devonport where she received major capability upgrades to her combat system and external communications equipment. The four boats are scheduled to decommission as follows: TORBAY (2017); TRENCHANT (2019); TALENT (2021) and TRIUMPH (2022).

AIRCRAFT CARRIER
QUEEN ELIZABETH CLASS

Ship	Pennant Number	Completion Date	Builder
QUEEN ELIZABETH	R08	2017	Aircraft Carrier Alliance
PRINCE OF WALES	*R09*	*2019*	*Aircraft Carrier Alliance*

Displacement 65,500 tons FL **Dimensions** 282.9m x 38.8m x 11m **Machinery** Integrated Full Electric Propulsion; 2 RR MT30 GT alternators, 93,870 hp (70 MW), 4 Wärtsilä DG, 53,064 hp (39.6 MW); 4 induction motors, 53,640 hp (40 MW); 2 shafts **Speed** 26 knots **Armament** 3 x Phalanx, 4 x 30mm **Aircraft** Up to 36 x F-35B Lightning and 4 x Merlin ASaC (Crowsnest). Typical mix could be 12-24 F-35B and various helicopters which could include Merlin, Chinook, Wildcat and Apache **Complement** 686 + 830 Air Group

Notes

As we closed for press QUEEN ELIZABETH was at an advanced state at its outfitting berth in Rosyth's inner basin. In the spring of 2017, QUEEN ELIZABETH is scheduled to complete safety and readiness checks before beginning an 11-week programme of sea trials in the North Sea on completion of which she will arrive at Portsmouth to begin an eight-week defect rectification period. First Of Class Flying Trials (Rotary Wing) are planned to run through the first quarter of 2018. These will be followed, towards the end of 2018, by First Of Class Flying Trials (Fixed Wing) off the US eastern seaboard with three fully instrumented F-35B test aircraft embarked. During 2019 and 2020 there will be further fixed-wing trials, work-up for the embarked battle staff, and building up the carrier strike group construct.

A contract for the construction of the two aircraft carriers, the largest warships to be designed and built in the UK, was signed in July 2008 between the Government and the Aircraft Carrier Alliance, an industrial group comprising BAE Systems Surface Ships, Babcock Marine, Thales and the Ministry of Defence.

The ships were built of sections constructed by BAE Systems at Govan, Scotstoun and Portsmouth; Babcock in Rosyth and Appledore; Cammell Laird in Birkenhead and A & P, Tyne and assembled in Number 1 Dock at Rosyth. The dock had the entrance widened from 124 feet to 138 feet. The sides were re-profiled with the removal of angled steps to make the dock floor 30 feet wider. A new overhead crane with a span of 394 feet, named Goliath, was installed to straddle the dock and lift the smaller blocks into place. The individual blocks are built under cover and fitted out with machinery and sub-assemblies such as diesel generators, offices, cabins and galleys before they are moved to Rosyth.

On 9 September 2015, Lower Block 03 (LB03) and Lower Block 02 (LB02) of the second ship, PRINCE OF WALES, were docked down into the build dock at Rosyth, marking the start of the assembly phase for PRINCE OF WALES. In October 2015 26,500t of the forward half of the ship was mechanically skidded back in the dry dock to the 12,000t superblock which makes up the rear of the vessel. Construction of the second ship is proceeding at a greater pace than the first. Construction of the 300m-long and 74m-wide vessel was completed in July 2016. Once QUEEN ELIZABETH leaves Rosyth it is expected that PRINCE OF WALES will be moved from the dry-dock to the fitting out berth. Following fitting out the ship is scheduled to begin sea trials in January 2019, followed by acceptance in August of the same year.

The aircraft carrier's flight deck has to be protected from the extreme temperatures produced by the Pratt & Whitney F135 engine fitted to the F-35B. A system developed by Monitor Coatings, uses a combination of aluminium and titanium to withstand temperatures of up to 1,500°C. The high cost of the coating, and the lengthy application process, mean that it is only being applied to selected areas of the flight deck. The thermal coating is applied using a specially developed twin wire arc technique, with the powdered metal fired through a jet of plasma at temperatures of almost 10,000°C. The molten droplets then flatten and quickly solidify, creating a resilient non-skid coating that is bonded to the steel beneath. However, application of the thermal metal spray must be undertaken at exactly the right rate in a controlled temperature environment. Approximately 2,000m^2 of the 19,000m^2 flight deck will be coated, comprising landing spots 2, 3 and 4, the intermediate runway between 3 and 4, and the runway spot 2 up to the 350 ft line.

Four personnel transfer boats are being built by Alnmaritec of Blyth (two for each carrier) These will be used to put crew ashore or transfer stores whilst at anchor or at sea. Of catamaran hull-form, the first to be delivered is named SWORDFISH.

HMS Ocean

LANDING PLATFORM HELICOPTER OCEAN

Ship	Pennant Number	Completion Date	Builder
OCEAN	L12	1998	Kvaerner

Displacement 22,500 tonnes Dimensions 203.8m x 35m x 6.6m Machinery 2 Crossley Pielstick diesels, 18,360 hp; 2 shafts; 1 bow thruster Speed 17 knots Armament 3 x Phalanx, 4 x 30mm ASC guns, 4 x Minigun Aircraft Tailored Air Group (Merlin, Sea King, Chinook, Apache as required) Complement Ship 285, Squadrons 206 (maximum 1275 including Royal Marines)

Notes

Can carry 12 Sea King and 6 Lynx helicopters. RAF Chinook helicopters are normally carried as an integral part of the ship's air group, but they are unable to be stowed below decks. Vessel is somewhat constrained by her slow speed. Many improvements have been made including accommodation for both crew and embarked Royal Marines; advanced communications facilities; a better weapon defence system and an upgrade to the ship's aviation support facilities to improve support to helicopter operations including the Apache attack helicopter. Scheduled to leave service in 2019, it has now been stated that she will decommission in 2018, without replacement. It is envisaged that one of the Queen Elizabeth class will undertake the LPH role as required.

HMS Bulwark

LANDING PLATFORM DOCK
ALBION CLASS

Ship	Pennant Number	Completion Date	Builder
ALBION	L14	2003	BAe Systems
BULWARK	L15	2004	BAe Systems

Displacement 18,500 tons, 21,500 tons (flooded) **Dimensions** 176m x 25.6m x 7.1m **Machinery** Diesel-electric; 2 Wärtsilä Vasa 32E DG, 17,000 hp (12.5 MW); 2 Wärtsilä Vasa 32LNE DG, 4,216 hp (3.1 MW); 2 motors; 2 shafts; 1 bow thruster **Speed** 18 knots **Armament** 2 x CIWS, 2 x 20mm guns (single) **Complement** 325 **Military Lift** 303 troops, with an overload capacity of a further 405

Notes

Vehicle deck capacity for up to six Challenger 2 tanks or around 30 armoured all-terrain tracked vehicles. Floodable well dock able to take four utility landing craft. Four smaller landing craft carried on davits. Two-spot flight deck able to take medium support helicopters and stow a third. Flight deck allows the simultaneous operation of two Chinook helicopters. These vessels do not have a hangar but have equipment needed to support aircraft operations. Only one of the class remains operational at this time. ALBION, which has been laid up since 2012 entered dry-dock in December 2014 to start a 30-month regeneration refit. Once complete, scheduled for April 2017, she will recommission and BULWARK will be placed at extended readiness. BULWARK is the last vessel in the fleet equipped with Goalkeeper. This will be replaced by Phalanx in both ships.

HMS Dragon

DESTROYERS
DARING CLASS (Type 45)

Ship	Pennant Number	Completion Date	Builder
DARING	D32	2008	BVT Surface Fleet
DAUNTLESS	D33	2008	BVT Surface Fleet
DIAMOND	D34	2009	BVT Surface Fleet
DRAGON	D35	2011	BVT Surface Fleet
DEFENDER	D36	2012	BVT Surface Fleet
DUNCAN	D37	2013	BVT Surface Fleet

Displacement 7,350 tons Dimensions 152.4m x 21.2m x 5.7m Machinery Integrated Electric Propulsion; 2 RR WR-21 GT alternators, 67,600 hp (49.7 MW); 2 Wärtsilä DG (4 MW); 2 Converteam motors (40 MW); 2 shafts Speed 29 knots Armament 1 - 4.5-inch gun, 2 x Quad Harpoon missile launchers (on four ships), Sea Viper missile system comprising Sylver VLS with combination of up to 48 Aster 15 and Aster 30 missiles, 2 x Vulcan Phalanx (fitted as required) Aircraft Lynx or Merlin Complement 190 (with space for 235)

Notes

Originally to have been a class of "up to" 12 ships this was reduced to just six. DRAGON was the first of the batch two destroyers, which include upgrades to systems onboard in line with technological developments. DAUNTLESS is operating as a Harbour Training Ship until her refit starts at the end of 2017.

The ships are capable of contributing to worldwide maritime and joint operations in multi threat environments and are primarily air defence ships. The Sea Viper missile ensures that the ships can destroy incoming threats from the air whilst the Sampson Multi-Function Radar can simultaneously detect and track over four hundred targets, providing a fully automatic operation where rapid reaction is required. In 2013 DARING participated in an anti-ballistic missile exercise with the US Navy in the Pacific to prove the Sampson radar in that mode. Although there are no plans to field an ABM missile, funding has been provided to demonstrate Sampson running ABM and AAW functions simultaneously. In order to give the ships an anti-ship capability the Harpoon missile systems removed from the decommissioned Batch III Type 22 frigates are being fitted to four of the Type 45 destroyers.

In June 2014 the MoD awarded BAE Systems a £70 million contract to manage the support, maintenance and upgrade of the Type 45 destroyers at Portsmouth Naval Base and on all their operations, both in the UK and globally.

The Type 45s have been dogged by availability and reliability shortfalls of the WR-21 GTA. This has severely impacted on the overall resilience of the Integrated Electric Propulsion system with total loss of ship propulsion and electrical power being a common occurrence. The main issue affecting reliability is the recuperator, which has proved insufficiently robust and prone to failure. Modifications have now been developed in order that WR-21 can now run at near full power without the recuperator, although there is a penalty to pay in terms of both fuel consumption (because the turbine is not benefitting from the recovery of exhaust energy) and mean failure rate. Rolls-Royce is currently progressing the development of a new, more reliable recuperator module. To overcome the issues Project Napier was established in 2014 with two core work strands. The Equipment Improvement Plan (EIP), is continuing efforts to enhance system reliability and to meet the original design intent in the near term while the longer term Power Improvement Plan (PIP) is intended to improve overall system resilience by adding upgraded diesel generators to provide the electrical generation capacity required to meet the overwhelming majority of propulsion and ship power requirements without reliance on WR-21. Various measures and modifications to the existing power and propulsion system have already been embodied, or are in the process of being introduced incrementally, under the EIP. The PIP project plans to deliver a diesel generator upgrade that will be embodied towards the end of the decade so as to add greater resilience to the power and propulsion system. Feasibility studies for this work, co-funded by BAE Systems and the MoD, concluded at the end of March 2015. The PIP is now into its assessment phase. The objective is to provide sufficient additional electrical generation capacity such that the IEP system can make cruise speeds (covering the major part of the Type 45 operating profile) on diesels alone. The WR-21 GTAs will remain to provide boost power as necessary, but will be used much less often.

The total cost and timetable of embodying the diesel generator upgrade will be determined at the main investment decision point.

FRIGATES

DUKE CLASS (Type 23)

Ship	Pennant Number	Completion Date	Builder
KENT	F78	2000	Yarrow
PORTLAND	F79	2000	Yarrow
SUTHERLAND	F81	1997	Yarrow
SOMERSET	F82	1996	Yarrow
ST ALBANS	F83	2001	Yarrow
LANCASTER	F229	1991	Yarrow
ARGYLL	F231	1991	Yarrow
IRON DUKE	F234	1992	Yarrow
MONMOUTH	F235	1993	Yarrow
MONTROSE	F236	1993	Yarrow
WESTMINSTER	F237	1993	Swan Hunter
NORTHUMBERLAND	F238	1994	Swan Hunter
RICHMOND	F239	1994	Swan Hunter

Displacement 4,900 tonnes Dimensions 133m x 16.1m x 5m Machinery CODLAG; 2 RR Spey GT, 31,100 hp (23.2 MW); 4 Paxman diesels 8,100 hp (6 MW); 2 GEC motors, 4,000 hp (3 MW); 2 shafts Speed 28 knots Armament Harpoon & Seawolf missile systems: 1 - 4.5-inch gun, 2 x single 30mm guns, 4 x magazine launched, Torpedo Tubes Aircraft Lynx or Merlin helicopter Complement 185

Notes

Now the sole class of frigate in RN service, the ships incorporate 'Stealth' technology to minimise magnetic, radar, acoustic and infra-red signatures. Gas turbine and diesel electric propulsion. Type 2087 Sonar is to be fitted in only 9 of the remaining 13 of the class (ARGYLL, MONTROSE, MONMOUTH and IRON DUKE will not receive the upgrade). LANCASTER is operating as a Harbour Training Ship until her refit begins in 2017.

The Type 996 surveillance and target indication radar has been replaced by the ARTI-SAN 3D Medium Range Radar (now designated Type 997) under a £100 million contract. The Type 997 is a modular open architecture maritime radar system designed to deal with complex littoral environments. It is being incrementally installed from 2011 as part of the Capability Sustainment Programme (CSP). The Seawolf missile system is expected to reach the end of its service life around 2018 and is being replaced by the Sea Ceptor as part of the Type 23 LIFEX refit bringing together CSP and extending the life of the hull and superstructure. WESTMINSTER and ARGYLL are expected to return to the fleet in 2017 fielding Sea Ceptor as the primary weapon system and MONTROSE is to receive the system during her current refit at Devonport.

In 2014 Babcock was awarded a contract to deliver an off-the-shelf Communications Electronic Support Measures (CESM) system to provide an enhanced electronic surveil-lance capability. The system, Hammerhead, will provide surveillance capability, sup-porting both tactical indicators and warnings and other tasked requirements. Babcock teamed with principal subcontractor Argon ST to deliver a system requiring no devel-opment work, to enable rapid replacement of the existing obsolete system on the Type 23s.

The MoD has also begun procurement activity to upgrade the power generation system, switchboards and machinery control and surveillance systems under the Power Generation and MCAS Update programme. On 7 August 2015 the MoD awarded a £68M contract, to Rolls-Royce subsidiary MTU, which includes a training and transitional sup-port package which will see each ship supplied with four new diesel generators and asso-ciated upgraded power distribution. A second contract, worth £12 million, went to Hitzinger UK, to provide voltage converters to deliver greater power to the frigates.

In September 2016 planned decommissioning dates were as follows: ARGYLL (2023); LAN-CASTER (2024); IRON DUKE (2025); MONMOUTH (2026); MONTROSE (2027); WESTMINSTER (2028); NORTHUMBERLAND (2029); RICHMOND (2030); SOMERSET (2031); SUTHERLAND (2032); KENT (2033); PORTLAND (2034) and ST. ALBANS (2035). In a debate about the Type 26 programme it was also revealed that it would not be possible to further extend the Type 23 out of service dates.

HMS Cattistock

MINE COUNTERMEASURES SHIPS (MCMV)
HUNT CLASS

Ship	Pennant Number	Completion Date	Builder
LEDBURY	M30	1981	Vosper T.
CATTISTOCK	M31	1982	Vosper T.
BROCKLESBY	M33	1983	Vosper T.
MIDDLETON	M34	1984	Yarrow
CHIDDINGFOLD	M37	1984	Vosper T.
ATHERSTONE	M38	1987	Vosper T.
HURWORTH	M39	1985	Vosper T.
QUORN	M41	1989	Vosper T.

Displacement 750 tonnes Dimensions 60m x 10.5m x 3.4m Machinery 2 Napier Deltic diesels or 2 Caterpillar C32 ACERT diesels; 1 Deltic 9-55B diesel for pulse generator and auxiliary drive; 2 shafts; 1 bow thruster Speed 15 knots Armament 1 x 30mm; 2 x Miniguns Complement 45

Notes

The largest warships ever built of glass reinforced plastic. Their cost (£35m each) has dictated the size of the class. Very sophisticated ships - and lively seaboats! All are based at Portsmouth as the Second Mine Countermeasures Squadron (MCM2).

BAE Systems has been awarded a six-year contract worth £15m to replace the propulsion systems on these ships, with the work to be carried out at Portsmouth. The first new propulsion system, comprising two Caterpillar C32 engines (replacing the older Napier Deltics) was installed on board CHIDDINGFOLD. Five such refits were completed by the end of 2016 (LEDBURY, CATTISTOCK, MIDDLETON, CHIDDINGFOLD and HURWORTH). The re-propulsion project will involve the installation of new engines, gearboxes, bow thruster systems, propellers and machinery control systems. BROCKLESBY was scheduled to return to the fleet in late 2016 following her refit. Due to changes applied to ship upkeep programmes, combined with the need to address emerging engineering issues work on the remaining vessels is now scheduled to complete in late 2019, rather than 2016 as originally planned.

Published decommissioning dates are LEDBURY (2019), CATTISTOCK, BROCKLESBY, CHID-DINGFOLD and MIDDLETON (2020), HURWORTH and ATHERSTONE (2022) and QUORN (2023). This is at odds with a press release from the RN on MIDDLETON's return to service in 2014 following her refit and diesel replacement. It was stated that *"the new engines mean that MIDDLETON can sail faster, stay at sea longer, and will extend the ship's life to 2030 and beyond"*. If this is the case it would appear that the Hunts will remain in service for quite some time with little hope of an immediate successor.

In order to keep up the overseas deployment tempo, crews are swapped between ships. MIDDLETON and CHIDDINGFOLD have been forward deployed to the Gulf since November 2015 and June 2014 respectively.

In 2013 the 9th MCM Squadron was stood up at Bahrain, comprising those vessels deployed to the Gulf in support of mine countermeasures operations. Those ships will be identified by a squadron funnel emblem depicting a traditional dhow, resurrecting the identity of the Ton class vessels deployed to the Gulf in the 1960s and 1970s as 9th MSS and latterly 9th MCMS.

As part of the wider Mine Countermeasures Hydrographic (MHC) programme – intended to deliver a replacement for the RN's mine warfare and hydrographic capabilities – the so-called MHC Sweep Capability project plans the introduction of a new remote control minesweeping system for deployment from the Hunt class, which lost its minesweeping capability when the sweep wires and associated equipment were removed in 2005. HAZARD, an optionally manned surface craft that will be able to venture into mine-fields to launch and recover unmanned underwater vehicles to search, locate and dispose of mines, can also be used to tow combined influence sweep gear. The concept is being tested by the Maritime Autonomous Systems Trials Team (MASTT) around Portsmouth. It is ultimately envisaged that a full scale demonstration, in the 2018-19 timeframe, could see a Hunt class converted for the launch and recovery of such vessels via an 'A' frame at the stern.

HMS Grimsby

SANDOWN CLASS

Ship	Pennant Number	Completion Date	Builder
PENZANCE	M106	1998	Vosper T.
PEMBROKE	M107	1998	Vosper T.
GRIMSBY	M108	1999	Vosper T.
BANGOR	M109	2000	Vosper T.
RAMSEY	M110	2000	Vosper T.
BLYTH	M111	2001	Vosper T.
SHOREHAM	M112	2001	Vosper T.

Displacement 600 tons Dimensions 52.5m x 109.m x 2m Machinery 2 Paxman Valenta diesels, 1,523 hp; Voith-Schneider propulsion; 2 bow thrusters Speed 13 knots Armament 1 x 30mm gun; 2 x Miniguns; 3 x GPMG Complement 34

Notes

A class dedicated to a single mine hunting role. Propulsion is by vectored thrust and bow thrusters. All are based at Faslane as the First Mine Countermeasures Squadron (MCM1). The ships are manned by eight numbered crews which are rotated throughout the squadron allowing deployed vessels to remain on station for extended periods. PENZANCE and BANGOR are forward deployed to the Gulf.

HMS Forth

PATROL VESSELS
RIVER II CLASS

Ship	Pennant Number	Completion Date	Builder
FORTH	P222	2017	BAE Systems
MEDWAY	P223	2017	BAE Systems
TRENT	P224	2018	BAE Systems

Displacement 2,000 tonnes **Dimensions** 90.5m x 13.5m x 3.8m **Speed** 25 knots **Armament** 1 x 30mm; 2 x Miniguns, 2 x GPMG **Aviation** Flight deck capable of receiving aircraft up to Merlin size **Complement** 34 (accommodation for 60)

Notes

Based on the 90m vessels in service with Brazil and Thailand, the basic design has been modified to meet specific RN requirements including a strengthened flight deck to operate a Merlin helicopter; modified and uprated helicopter in-flight refuelling arrangements; additional accommodation for embarked military detachments and improved watertight integrity and firefighting equipment. The ships will feature BAE's CMS-1 combat management system, an I Band Doppler SharpEye radar for helicopter control and navigation and an E/F Band SharpEye radar for navigation and collision avoidance. FORTH is expected to be handed over in spring 2017. MEDWAY, will be delivered in October 2017 and TRENT in July 2018. A further two vessels, as yet un-named, are to be ordered and likely to be handed over to the RN by 2019. It is likely that this class will conduct global operations in addition to UK patrol tasks.

● DANIEL FERRO   HMS Mersey

RIVER CLASS

Ship	Pennant Number	Completion Date	Builder
TYNE	P281	2002	Vosper T.
SEVERN	P282	2003	Vosper T.
MERSEY	P283	2003	Vosper T.

Displacement 1,677 tonnes Dimensions 79.5m x 13.6m x 3.8m Machinery 2 MAN 12RK 270 diesels, 11,063 hp; 2 shafts; bow thruster Speed 20+ knots Armament 1 x 20mm; 2 x GPMG Complement 48

Notes

Ordered on 8 May 2001, the deal was unusual in that the ships were leased from Vospers (VT) for five years under a £60 million contract. In January 2007 a £52 million lease-contract extension was awarded extending their RN service to the end of 2013. In September 2012 Whitehall signed a £39m contract to buy the ships outright, keeping them in service with the RN for the next ten years. The River class are now the only RN ships permanently conducting Fishery Protection patrols in the waters around England, Wales and Northern Ireland. Both SEVERN and MERSEY have undertaken six-month deployments to the Caribbean as part of the Atlantic Patrol Task (North). Although this class could remain operational until 2022, it has been confirmed that they will be replaced by the River II class vessels.

HMS Clyde

RIVER CLASS OPV(H)

Ship	Pennant Number	Completion Date	Builder
CLYDE	P257	2006	VT Shipbuilding

Displacement 1,847 tonnes Dimensions 81.5m x 13.6m x 4.15m Machinery 2 MAN 12RK 270 diesels, 11,063 hp; 2 shafts; bow thruster Speed 19 knots (full load) 21 knots (sprint) Aircraft Flight Deck to take Lynx, Sea King or Merlin Helicopter Armament 1 x 30mm gun; 5 x GPMG; 2 x Minigun Complement 36 (space for additional 20 personnel - see note)

Notes

Permanently deployed to the South Atlantic, CLYDE was designed to carry out patrol duties around the Falkland Islands and their dependencies. The ship is able to accommodate a single helicopter up to Merlin size. She is also able to embark a Military Force of up to 110 personnel (the size of the Roulement Infantry Company (RIC)) and move them around the Falkland Islands, inserting them at will. Like the previous River class, she had been leased from BAE Systems, for a period of five years. In July 2011 it was announced that BAE Systems had been awarded a six-year contract extension to deliver support services to the ship until 2018. The annual cost to the public purse of operating the ship is £3.5 million. She is to be replaced by one of the new River II class.

HMS Sabre

SCIMITAR CLASS

Ship	Pennant Number	Completion Date	Builder
SCIMITAR	P284	1988	Halmatic
SABRE	P285	1988	Halmatic

Displacement 18.5 tons **Dimensions** 16m x 4.7m x 1.4m **Machinery** 2 MAN V10 diesels, 740 hp; 2 shafts **Speed** 27+ knots **Armament** 2 x GPMG **Complement** 4

Notes

Assigned to the Royal Navy Gibraltar Squadron (RNGS) the vessels provide Force Protection to visiting warships, maritime security patrols within British Gibraltar Territorial Waters and support a variety of operations within the Joint Operating Area. In recent years the craft have been facing increasingly provocative stand-offs with their Spanish counterparts in the Guardia Civil as Spain tries to assert its influence over, what it views as, disputed waters in the Bay of Gibraltar. In response additional RN personnel have been deployed to Gibraltar, increasing the number of crews from two to three. RNGS also operate up to three Rigid Hull Inflatable Boats supported by two 15 metre launches and three Arctic 24 RHIBS operated by the Gibraltar Defence Police.

HMS Exploit

COASTAL TRAINING CRAFT
P2000 CLASS

Ship	Pennant Number	Completion Date	Builder
EXPRESS	P163	1988	Vosper T.
EXPLORER	P164	1985	Watercraft
EXAMPLE	P165	1985	Watercraft
EXPLOIT	P167	1988	Vosper T.
ARCHER	P264	1985	Watercraft
BITER	P270	1985	Watercraft
SMITER	P272	1986	Watercraft
PURSUER	P273	1988	Vosper T.
TRACKER	P274	1998	Ailsa Troon
RAIDER	P275	1998	Ailsa Troon
BLAZER	P279	1988	Vosper T.
DASHER	P280	1988	Vosper T.

Ship	Pennant Number	Completion Date	Builder
PUNCHER	P291	1988	Vosper T.
CHARGER	P292	1988	Vosper T.
RANGER	P293	1988	Vosper T.
TRUMPETER	P294	1988	Vosper T.

Displacement 54 tonnes Dimensions 20m x 5.8m x 1.9m Machinery 2 RR CV 12 M8000T diesels, 1,590 hp; 2 MTU diesels, 2,000 hp (TRACKER); All to be replaced by Caterpillar C18 diesels, 1,746 hp; 2 shafts Speed 20 knots Armament 3 x GPMG (Faslane based vessels) Complement 5 (with accommodation for up to 12 undergraduates).

Notes

Fourteen P2000 craft form the First Patrol Boat Squadron, whose primary role is to support the University Royal Naval Units (URNU) but also contribute to a wide range of Fleet tasking. Commodore Britannia Royal Naval College has overall responsibility for the URNUs whose role is to educate and inform a wide spectrum of high calibre undergraduates. Vessels are assigned to the following URNUs: ARCHER (East Scotland); BITER (Manchester & Salford); BLAZER (Southampton); CHARGER (Liverpool); DASHER (Bristol); EXAMPLE (Northumbria); EXPLOIT (Birmingham); EXPLORER (Yorkshire); EXPRESS (Wales); PUNCHER (London); PURSUER (Glasgow & Strathclyde); RANGER (Sussex); SMITER (Oxford); TRUMPETER (Cambridge).

The last two vessels built, RAIDER and TRACKER, comprise the Faslane Patrol Boat Squadron. They are fully-fledged armed patrol boats. Fitted with Kevlar armour and able to mount three 7.62mm General Purpose Machine Guns (GPMG) they are part of a growing Force Protection cadre based at Faslane to protect the UKs nuclear deterrent. These two vessels are fully engaged in FP duties and do not undertake university training.

The P2000s engines are being replaced by two CAT C18 Acert units to help reduce emissions, lower fuel consumption and improve efficiency. BITER was the first to be fitted during an extended refit, followed by EXPLORER, RANGER, EXPRESS, ARCHER and RAIDER. The latest, CHARGER, was returned to the RN in October 2016.

HMS Scott

SURVEY SHIPS
SCOTT CLASS

Ship	Pennant Number	Completion Date	Builder
SCOTT	H131	1997	Appledore

Displacement 13,300 tonnes **Dimensions** 131.5m x 21.5m x 9m **Machinery** 2 Krupp MaK 9M32 diesels, 10,800 hp; 1 shaft, CP propellor; retractable bow thruster **Speed** 17 knots **Complement** 63 (42 embarked at any one time)

Notes

Designed to commercial standards SCOTT provides the RN with a deep bathymetric capability off the continental shelf. Fitted with a modern multi-beam sonar suite she can conduct mapping of the ocean floor worldwide. She carries a mixture of the latest UK and US survey equipment. She operates a three watch system whereby the vessel is run by 42 of her ship's company of 63 - with the remainder on leave. Each crew member works 75 days in the ship before having 30 days ashore for leave, training and other duties, allowing her to spend more than 300 days at sea in a year. Her hull is Ice class 1A: Ships with such structure, engine output and other properties are capable of navigating in difficult ice conditions, but only with the assistance of icebreakers. In 2013 Babcock won a five year contract from the MoD to provide through life engineering support to the ship. Following an extensive refit in 2015 the ship deployed for nine-months conducting survey operations all over the North Atlantic and Mediterranean. She returned to Plymouth in March 2016 for leave and maintenance prior to deploying once more in the summer.

HMS Echo

ECHO CLASS

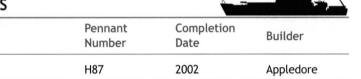

Ship	Pennant Number	Completion Date	Builder
ECHO	H87	2002	Appledore
ENTERPRISE	H88	2003	Appledore

Displacement 3,500 tonnes Dimensions 90m x 16.8m x 5.5.m Machinery Diesel electric; 3 DG (4.8MW); 2 azimuth thrusters, 2,279 hp (1.7 MW); 1 bow thruster Speed 15 knots Armament 2 x 20mm Complement 49 (with accommodation for 81)

Notes

In June 2000, a £130 million order was placed with prime contractor Vosper Thornycroft to build and maintain, over a 25 year period, these two new Survey Vessels Hydrographic Oceanographic (SVHO). Both vessels were built by sub-contractor Appledore Shipbuilding Limited. They have a secondary role as mine countermeasures HQ ships. The total ship's company is 72, with 48 personnel onboard at any one time working a cycle of 75 days on, 30 days off, allowing the ships to be operationally available for 330 days a year. Utilizing a diesel electric propulsion system, they have three main generators. They are the first RN ships to be fitted with Azimuth pod thrusters in place of the more normal shaft and propellor. Each ship carries a named survey launch, SAPPHIRE (ECHO) and SPITFIRE (ENTERPRISE), equipped with side scan sonar and both multi-beam and single beam echo sounders. ENTERPRISE remains deployed in support of the EU mission to tackle the migration crisis in the Mediterranean. As of January 2016 ECHO augmented the Fishery Protection Squadron while MERSEY was deployed to the Caribbean.

HMS Gleaner

INSHORE SURVEY VESSEL

Ship	Pennant Number	Completion Date	Builder
GLEANER	H86	1983	Emsworth

Displacement 26 tons Dimensions 14.8m x 4.7m x 1.6m Machinery 2 Volvo Penta TMD 112 diesels, 524 hp; 2 shafts Speed 14 knots Complement 8

Notes

Small inshore survey craft used for the collection of data from the shallowest inshore waters. She uses multi-beam and sidescan sonar to collect bathymetry and seabed texture data and compile an accurate and detailed picture of the seabed. She was scheduled to decommission in 2007, but emerged, in 2008, from a Service Life Extension Programme, which will enable her to remain in service for a further 10 years. She carries the prefix Her Majesty's Survey Motor Launch or HMSML. In 2016 she spent several weeks surveying the Forth estuary to ensure carrier HMS QUEEN ELIZABETH would be able to leave Rosyth dockyard for her scheduled sea trials in the spring of 2017.

Four small survey boats, NESBITT, PAT BARTON, COOK and OWEN are attached to the Hydrographic School at Devonport.

ICE PATROL SHIP
PROTECTOR

Ship	Pennant Number	Completion Date	Builder
PROTECTOR	A173	2001	Havyard Leirvik (Norway)

Displacement 4,985 tons Dimensions 89.7m x 18m x 7.25m Machinery 2 Bergen diesels, 9,602 hp; 1 shaft; CP propellor; bow and stern thrusters Speed 15 knots Armament Miniguns; GPMGs Complement 88

Notes

The ice-breaker MV POLARBJØRN was initially leased, in June 2011, on a three-year contract from the Norwegian company GC Rieber Shipping as a temporary replacement for the damaged ENDURANCE and commissioned as PROTECTOR. In 2013 it was announced that the ship had been purchased by the MoD.

Although the ship has a flight deck, there is no hangar, so she is unable to deploy with an embarked helicopter. However, for her latest deployment the ship has been given three 3D-printed micro-aircraft, identical to one tested on board HMS MERSEY in 2015 off the Dorset coast. The aircraft are controlled from a laptop on board, can cruise at nearly 60 mph and are all but noiseless thanks to their tiny engine. Each one costs no more than

£7,000 – cheaper than an hour's flying time by a Fleet Air Arm helicopter. Each micro-aircraft can fly for up to 30 minutes, recording video footage on a miniscule camera, before setting down in the icy waters or on the snow and ice where it will be picked up by PROTECTOR's ship's company.

She also operates the Survey Motor Boat JAMES CAIRD IV and the 8.5 metre Rigid Work Boat TERRA NOVA. She can also deploy two Pacific 22 RIBs (NIMROD and AURORA). She also deploys with three BV206 all terrain vehicles and four quad bikes and trailers to assist in moving stores and equipment. In 2015, the ship changed her base port from Portsmouth, to join the rest of the Hydrographic Squadron at Devonport.

The ship sailed for her latest deployment in October 2015, but rather than operating in her more traditional waters of the South Atlantic, the ship headed east, visiting the Seychelles and Australia before embarking on survey operations in the Ross Sea, which has not been visited by a Royal Navy vessel for 80 years. The ship has eight different 'work packages' planned in and around Antarctica. Those spells of intensive work, making use of the warmer temperatures and less inclement weather of the Austral summer, will focus on updating charts of the waters for the UK Hydrographic Office, monitoring wildlife and assisting the work of international inspectors who visit the numerous scientific bases peppered around the Antarctic.

The ship is scheduled to be away from the UK until the spring of 2017. One third of her crew rotates every few weeks to sustain the ship on operations.

The Survey Motor Boat JAMES CAIRD IV (Daniel Ferro)

ROYAL MARINE CRAFT

RM Tamar, a newly built facility, housed at Devonport Naval Base, is home to the RMs Landing Craft, Hovercraft and other vessels when not required for deployment, either onboard the assault ships, or independently.

Based at RM Tamar is 1 Assault Group Royal Marines (1 AGRM), the lead for amphibious warfare and Royal Navy board and search training. The group is tasked with training and developing core amphibious and surface assault skills and equipment, including the provision of operational support for the Ministry of Defence.

1 AGRM is responsible for 4 subordinate units which deliver the vast spectrum of training and operations required in delivering amphibious and surface assault capability of the Royal Navy and Royal Marines.

10 (Landing Craft) Training Squadron - Responsible for delivering landing craftsmen training as well as small boats, engineering and assault navigation training.

11 Amphibious Trials and Training Squadron (Instow, North Devon) - Delivering training that covers the area between the craft and the beachhead. The Instow squadron also conducts the trials and testing of future craft.

The Royal Navy School of Board and Search at HMS Raleigh in Torpoint trains both individuals and ship's boarding teams to conduct the full range of boarding operations that is required by the Naval Service.

In addition, 1AGRM is also tasked with parenting the Assault Squadrons of the Royal Marines (ASRMs) and their Landing Craft detachments which are assigned to the amphibious assault ships. These ASRMs provide the landing craft and therefore the fighting capability for the RN's Amphibious Ships, OCEAN (9 ASRM); ALBION (6 ASRM - currently disbanded and operated as 6 Ops Sqn until ALBION returns to service) and BULWARK (4 ASRM).

43 Commando Fleet Protection Group Royal Marines (43 Cdo FP Gp RM) is based at HM Naval Base Clyde near Helensburgh on the West Coast of Scotland. Formerly Comacchio Group it was renamed in April 2012 and, together with 539 ASRM, became part of 3 Commando Brigade. The Group's core task is to provide military support to undertake final denial of access to nuclear weapons in addition to supporting the multi-agency force that protects nuclear weapons convoys. Additionally, specially trained teams are deployed at short notice to conduct tasks in support of the RN worldwide. Tasks have ranged from Force Protection, to conducting non-compliant boarding operations and counter-piracy operations.

Mull

ISLAND CLASS PATROL VESSELS

Ship	Pennant Number	Launch Date	Builder
RONA	-	2009	Holyhead Marine
MULL	-	2010	Holyhead Marine
EORSA	-	2014	Holyhead Marine

Displacement 19.9 tonnes **Dimensions** 14.9m x 4.6m x 0.9m **Machinery** 2 Caterpillar diesels, 715 hp; 2 waterjets **Speed** 33 knots **Armament** 4 x GPMG **Complement** 4

Notes

RONA and MULL were former Ministry of Defence Police vessels. They were fitted with three new weapons mounts, extra protection and communications equipment and transferred to 43 Commando Fleet Protection Group Royal Marines for operation on the Clyde to escort high value units. A third vessel, EORSA, was delivered direct from the builders. The MoD Police operate nine other vessels in the class, GIGHA, JURA, HARRIS, LEWIS, SKYE, LISMORE, IONA, BARRA and TIREE.

LCU Mk10 A2

LCU Mk10

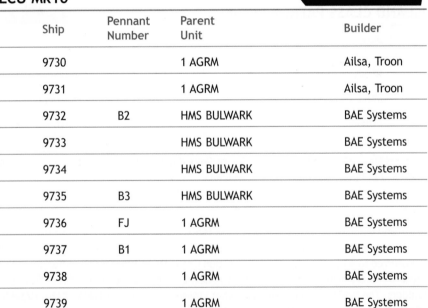

Ship	Pennant Number	Parent Unit	Builder
9730		1 AGRM	Ailsa, Troon
9731		1 AGRM	Ailsa, Troon
9732	B2	HMS BULWARK	BAE Systems
9733		HMS BULWARK	BAE Systems
9734		HMS BULWARK	BAE Systems
9735	B3	HMS BULWARK	BAE Systems
9736	FJ	1 AGRM	BAE Systems
9737	B1	1 AGRM	BAE Systems
9738		1 AGRM	BAE Systems
9739		1 AGRM	BAE Systems

Displacement 240 tonnes   Dimensions 29.82m x 7.7m x 1.70m   Machinery 2 MAN Diesels; 2 Schottel propulsors; 1 bow thruster   Speed 8.5 knots   Armament 2 x GPMG Complement 7

Notes

Ro-Ro style landing craft designed to operate from the Albion class LPDs or Landing Ship Dock Auxiliary (LSD(A)). Ordered in 1998 from Ailsa Troon. The first two were delivered in 1999 with the final vessels being accepted into service in 2003. The remainder were built by BAE Systems at Govan. Capable of lifting one Main Battle Tank or four lighter vehicles. Capacity for 100 fully equipped troops. With a range of around 600 nautical miles – more if auxiliary tanks are added – they are designed to operate independently for 14 days with a seven man Royal Marine crew in both arctic and tropical climates. All the crew members have bunk accommodation and there is a galley and store rooms. Unlike other vessels, pennant numbers and parent units can change as the vessels are rotated through maintenance cycles.

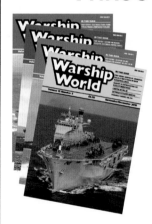

LCVP Mk5B 0356

LCVP Mk5B

Ship	Pennant Number	Parent Unit	Builder
0202	B5	HMS BULWARK	Babcock Marine
0203	NM	HMS OCEAN	Babcock Marine
0204	B6	HMS BULWARK	Babcock Marine
0205	P7	1 AGRM	Babcock Marine
0338	T6	1 AGRM	Babcock Marine
0339		HMS OCEAN	Babcock Marine
0340	N2	HMS OCEAN	Babcock Marine
0341		1 AGRM	Babcock Marine
0344		1 AGRM	Babcock Marine
0345		1 AGRM	Babcock Marine
0346	N3	HMS OCEAN	Babcock Marine

Ship	Pennant Number	Parent Unit	Builder
0347		HMS BULWARK	Babcock Marine
0353		HMS BULWARK	Babcock Marine
0354		1 AGRM	Babcock Marine
0355		1 AGRM	Babcock Marine
0356	B8	1 AGRM	Babcock Marine

Displacement 24 tonnes Dimensions 15.70m x 3.5m x 0.90m Machinery 2 Volvo Penta diesels; 2 waterjets Speed 25 knots Armament 2 x GPMG Complement 3

Notes

First one ordered in 1995 from Vosper Thornycroft and handed over in 1996. A further four were delivered in December 1996 to operate from OCEAN, with two more for training at RM Poole ordered in 1998. A further 16 were ordered from Babcock in 2001 with the final vessels being accepted into service in 2004. The Mk 5 can lift 8 tonnes of stores or a mix of 2 tonnes and 35 troops. These vessels have a greater range, lift and speed than the Mk4s which they replaced. The primary role is the landing of vehicles, personnel and equipment onto potentially hostile shores. The secondary role is a general purpose support craft both between ships and ship to shore. The craft are capable of performing normal duties in conditions up to sea state 4 and run for cover up to sea state 5. Pennant numbers and parent units can change as the vessels are rotated through maintenance cycles.

LCVP Mk5A 9707, 9675 and 9676, listed in the previous edition, are to be withdrawn from service in January 2017.

GRIFFON 2400TD LCAC

Ship	Pennant Number	Completion Date	Builder
C21	-	2010	Griffon
C22	-	2010	Griffon
C23	-	2010	Griffon
C24	-	2010	Griffon

G.R.T. 6.8 tons Dimensions 13.4m x 6.8m Machinery 1 Deutz diesel, 585 hp Speed 45 knots Range 300 nm Armament 1 x GPMG Complement 2 Crew; 16 fully-equipped marines.

Notes

Operated by 539 Assault Squadron, the 2400TD offers greater payload, performance and obstacle clearance than the earlier 2000 TD craft. Centre sections of the cabin roof can be removed in order to embark two one-tonne NATO pallets. They can be transported on a standard low loader truck or in the hold of a C-130 Hercules aircraft. They can also operate directly from the well-deck of RN amphibious ships. They are equipped with a 7.62mm General Purpose Machine Gun, HF and VHF radios, radar, GPS, ballistic protection and a variety of specialised equipment. All four entered service by the end of 2010.

OFFSHORE RAIDING CRAFT

The Royal Marines operate two versions of the Offshore Raiding Craft (ORC), the Troop Carrying Variant (TCV) and Fire Support Variant (FSV). The ORC is an air portable surface manoeuvre craft designed for the rapid deployment of 8 fully equipped troops and 2 crew from over the horizon (30 miles) ship to shore and vice versa. They provide rapid movement of troops in coastal, estuarine, riverine and inland waters. Specifications: Weight: 3.6 tonnes - Length: 9.1m - Speed: 36 kts - Capacity: 2 Crew + 8 fully equipped troops.

RIGID RAIDING CRAFT

The Royal Marines operate a number of smaller Rigid-hulled and Rigid-Inflatable craft for various assault, patrol and security duties. There are 5.2, 6.5 and 8 metre long versions. Rigid Raiders feature GRP (glass reinforced plastic) hulls and early variants featured single or twin outboard motors. The latest RRC, the Mk3, is powered by an inboard diesel engine. They can carry up to eight troops.

SPECIALIST CRAFT

In addition to the familiar Rigid Raiding Craft and Rigid Inflatable Boats other specialist vessels are available including air transportable Fast Insertion Craft (FIC) with a speed of 55 knots in addition to advanced wave piercing designs. Swimmer Delivery Vehicles (SDV), in reality miniature submarines, which can be deployed from dry deck shelters on larger submarines, are also operated as a part of the UK Special Forces inventory.

Following trials with Swedish CP90 Combat Boats, the Royal Marines were hopeful of procuring a new Force Protection Craft, based on experience with the CB 90s, capable of landing troops and protecting the landing craft from seaborne and land based threats. An in service date of 2016 was anticipated, but to date there has been little indication of progress with this programme.

SHIPS FOR THE FUTURE FLEET

BAE SYSTEMS

TYPE 26 FRIGATE (GLOBAL COMBAT SHIP)

Conceived as a multi-mission warship designed for joint and multi-national operations across the full spectrum of warfare, the Type 26 is planned to progressively replace the Type 23 frigates from the early part of the next decade. It was planned that 13 ships were to replace the current Type 23s on a one-for-one basis but there had also been mention of a class of "up to" 13 ships. SDSR 2015 confirmed that the Type 26 programme would comprise just eight ships, replacing the ASW capable Type 23s, while a further class of lighter frigate would be acquired to replace the general purpose ships - indications were that this class could exceed five in number.

The Type 26 will employ a Combined Diesel Electric or Gas Turbine propulsion system. This will enable the ships to achieve high speeds, whilst also providing an economic power to the onboard systems and will allow the ships to operate quietly in cruising mode. Rolls-Royce has been selected as the design partner for Gas Turbines, while David Brown Gear Systems Ltd will develop the Gear-box and MTU the Diesel Generator Sets. Rohde & Schwarz has been selected to design the Integrated Communications System for the ships. In July 2016 BAE systems was awarded a £183 million contract to provide three Maritime Indirect Fires Systems (MIFS), Integrated Gunnery System (IGS) and one trainer system for the RN. The MIFS IGS includes the 5-inch/62 calibre Mk45 gun along with an automated ammunition handling system, a fire control system and ammunition. The contract includes an option for five other systems for the remainder of the class. It is also likely that the Lockheed Martin Mk 41 VLS system will be selected to meet the requirement for a 24-cell Flexible Strike Silo. The ship will be able to support Wildcat or Merlin helicopters as well as having a flightdeck capable of landing a Chinook with the ramp down to embark troops. Forward of the hangar

43

will be a mission bay enabling the ship to carry differing payloads depending on operational requirements.

The Assessment Phase for the Type 26 programme began in March 2010, with a Main Investment decision by the end of 2014, but this was delayed until after the Scottish independence referendum. In February 2015, the MoD and BAE Systems signed a contract worth £859m to continue development, supporting progression towards the manufacturing phase. In March 2016 BAE was awarded a further £472 million contract to progress the Type 26 programme. Key equipment purchases include diesel generators, sonar domes for the bow-mounted sonar and helicopter ground handling equipment and arrangements. Other equipment includes mission bay side doors, for the loading/unloading of equipment,stabiliser and steering gear system and key elements of the T26 navigation system. Effective from April 2016, the 15 month contract extends the current demonstration phase and allows for the manufacturing of equipment necessary for construction of the first three ships.

Manufacture of the ships was scheduled to start in 2016 with the first vessel due to enter service in the early 2020s. The construction phase has, however, been delayed sparking various reports citing that either the MoD had no money for the programme; that the design had not been finalised or that the MoD were squeezing BAE for a more competitive price. In October 2016 it was finally announced that first steel will be cut in the summer of 2017 subject to final contract negotiations.

THE GENERAL PURPOSE FRIGATE (TYPE 31)

It would appear that the precise details of the General Purpose Frigate (Type 31), as outlined in SDSR 2015, have yet to be determined. It was announced that the RN would acquire a class of lighter more affordable frigates, possibly in greater numbers than the five Type 23 frigates they are to replace. Perceived by many to be a modern day Type 21 - a light weight 'off the shelf' there seems little clear direction at the moment. There is some early pre-concept work underway in Naval Command HQ and the MoD but there has been, to date, no formal guidance as to where the ship will sit on the cost/capability curve.

Several options are available. Type 31 could be built on the same hull as the Type 26 but with different engines and weapons. The vessel could be brought off the shelf using a commercial design such as BMTs Venator 110 light frigate or a stretched version of BAEs own Project Khareef corvette as built for the Royal Navy of Oman. The design could be as basic as a stretched River class OPV.

Given the out of service dates of the Type 23 class and the statement that there can be no life extension of the Type 23s beyond these dates, both the Type 26 and Type 31 programmes will have to deliver to a very tight build schedule.

A notional FSS design developed by the combined MoD/Industry Naval Design Partnering team

MILITARY AFLOAT REACH AND SUSTAINABILITY (MARS)

The future re-equipment of the RFA rests with this programme which initially envisioned the procurement of five fleet tankers; three joint sea-based logistics vessels; two fleet solid-support ships and a single fleet tanker.

Post SDSR 2010 the government stated that the requirement for the MARS programme was driven by the logistic support needs of the future RN. It now seems likely that MARS will deliver just seven vessels (four Tide class and up to three solid-support ships).

In February 2012 the MoD announced that Daewoo Shipbuilding and Marine Engineering (DSME) of South Korea were the preferred bidder in a £425 million contract to build the four Tide class tankers for the RFA, the first of which is planned to enter service this year (see page 50).

With the tanker programme now under contract, the MoD is turning its attention towards the other MARS component in the shape of the Future Solid Support (FSS) programme. This second element of the modernisation of the RFA is intended to introduce replacements for RFAs FORT AUSTIN, FORT ROSALIE and FORT VICTORIA from the early 2020s.

SDSR 2015 announced the planned acquisition of three FSS ships to enter service from the mid-2020s. The ships will be required to deliver ammunition and stores at a tempo and volume needed to support carrier strike operations. In advance of starting the FSS procurement the MoD has already contracted Rolls-Royce to develop, test and prove a new generation Heavy Replenishment at Sea rig (HRAS) that will allow transfer of up to 5-tonnes at a time. The land based demonstrator has completed successful trials and is now installed at HMS Raleigh as part of a new RAS training facility.

The FSS programme is going through the MoD approvals process in order to progress to the Assessment Phase. Like the Tide class tankers, the FSS have been classified as non-warlike and as a result it is likely that the acquisition programme will be opened up to international competition.

BAE SYSTEMS

SUCCESSOR SUBMARINE PROGRAMME

The Successor programme envisages the delivery of four SSBNs to replace the RN's four existing Vanguard-class submarines from 2028 to maintain Continuous At-Sea Deterrence (CASD). Initial gate approval was announced by the MoD in May 2011, marking the transition from the programme's concept phase to the assessment phase. Assessment phase activities will finalise the Successor design, fund long lead items and start industrialisation to support manufacture.

Work on the concept design phase for a submarine to replace the Vanguard class has been ongoing since 2007 and an outline submarine design has been selected. Work with the US on a Common Missile Compartment is ongoing to evaluate how best to incorporate the UK's requirement for eight operational missiles, against a baseline design for the CMC which currently involves a 12 missile tube unit. It has been recognised that the cost of the CMC will be minimised by keeping as much of the design as possible in common with the US.

In 2012 two contracts worth £350 million each were awarded by the MoD to enable detailed design work to continue on both the submarine design and the new PWR3 nuclear reactor. In March 2015 BAE Systems was awarded additional funding of £257 million to cover the final phase of work. In February 2016 a further £201 million package was announced to support further design work and in March a £642 million investment towards further design, new parts and facilities at Barrow, taking the total cost of the Assessment phase to £3.9 billion.

At the end of March 2016 the government put its case for retaining the deterrent and won the backing of Parliament. In October it was announced that construction work was to start on the new submarines with £1.3 billion of new investment to move the programme to the Delivery phase with manufacturing work beginning on structural steel for the first submarine. At 152.9m (501ft) long, the new boats will be three metres longer than their predecessors, and displace 1,300 tonnes more. It was announced on 21 October, that the first boat is to be named DREADNOUGHT. Such historical resonance will continue through the names of boats 2, 3 and 4.

THE ROYAL FLEET AUXILIARY

The Royal Fleet Auxiliary (RFA) is a civilian manned fleet, owned by the Ministry of Defence. Traditionally, its main task has been to replenish warships of the Royal Navy at sea with fuel, food, stores and ammunition to extend their operations away from base support. However, as the RN surface fleet has shrunk, the RFA has shrunk with it but it has also acted as a 'force multiplier' being able to take on some operational roles. By embarking helicopters, tankers and stores ships have been deployed on RN patrol tasks in the Caribbean, on counter-piracy operations in the Indian Ocean and, more recently, on operations in the eastern Mediterranean in support of the migrant crisis. By embarking ASW helicopters they are also able to provide additional warfare support to task group operations. Like the RN, the RFA are suffering manpower shortages, particularly in the engineering specialisation, and it has been noticeable that ships are spending extended periods alongside, reportedly laid-up due to lack of engineering staff. Although the MoD state that those ships remain in the operational cycle, ORANGELEAF was withdrawn from service, whilst laid up, and towed away for scrap in 2016; BLACK ROVER remains laid up at Birkenhead, unlikely to return to sea and the repair ship DILIGENCE was withdrawn from service and put up for sale in 2016, well ahead of her declared 2020 out of service date.

The loss of DILIGENCE, without replacement creates another capability gap although the government stress that she was one part of a system providing support facilities to deployed RN ships and submarines. This support, they say, is regularly supplemented by commercial arrangements and international agreements and when bespoke afloat capabilities are required, these are contracted on the open market.

As part of the Military Afloat Reach and Sustainability (MARS) programme, the MoD placed an order in 2012 for four tankers to be built in South Korea. The first of class, TIDESPRING, was expected to enter service in 2016, but technical issues have resulted in the ship being delayed until 2017. As a result GOLD ROVER, which was to have returned from deployment in 2016, will not now return until 2017.

The long term maintenance of the RFA fleet rests with shipyards in the North West, North East and South West of England. Cammell Laird Shiprepairers & Shipbuilders Ltd of Birkenhead and the A&P Group in Falmouth and Newcastle-upon-Tyne were named as the contractors to maintain the flotilla of 11v RFA tankers, stores and landing ships. They maintain 'clusters' of ships, providing the necessary refuelling and refit work for the RFA vessels throughout their service lives. Ships are grouped in clusters according to their duties and capabilities. A&P Group are charged with two clusters (Cluster 1: ARGUS and Cluster 2: CARDIGAN BAY, LYME BAY, MOUNTS BAY) in a contract worth around £53 million with the work to be shared between its bases in Falmouth and on the Tyne, while CL Ltd is contracted for the maintenance of four clusters of ships (Cluster 3: BLACK ROVER, GOLD ROVER; Cluster 4: WAVE KNIGHT, WAVE RULER; Cluster 5: FORT AUSTIN, FORT ROSALIE and Cluster 6: FORT VICTORIA).

SHIPS OF THE ROYAL FLEET AUXILIARY
Pennant Numbers

Ships	P. No.	Page	Ships	P. No.	Page
Tankers			Stores Ship/Tankers		
TIDESPRING	A136	50	FORT VICTORIA	A387	53
TIDERACE	*A137*	*50*			
TIDESURGE	*A138*	*50*	Amphibious Ships		
TIDEFORCE	*A139*	*50*			
GOLD ROVER	A271	51	LYME BAY	L3007	54
BLACK ROVER	A273	51	MOUNTS BAY	L3008	54
WAVE KNIGHT	A389	49	CARDIGAN BAY	L3009	54
WAVE RULER	A390	49			
			Primary Casualty Receiving		
Stores Ships			Ship/Aviation Training Ship		
FORT ROSALIE	A385	52	ARGUS	A135	55
FORT AUSTIN	A386	52			

FAST FLEET TANKERS
WAVE CLASS

Ship	Pennant Number	Completion Date	Builder
WAVE KNIGHT	A389	2002	BAe Systems
WAVE RULER	A390	2002	BAe Systems

Displacement 31,500 tons (FL) Dimensions 196m x 27m x 10m Machinery Diesel-electric; 4 Wärtsilä DG, 25,514 hp (18.76 MW); 2 GEC Alstom motors with variable speed converters, 19,040 hp (14 MW); 1 shaft; 1 bow and stern thruster Speed 18 knots Armament 2 x Vulcan Phalanx, 2 x 30mm Aircraft Up to 2 Merlin Complement 80 (plus 22 Fleet Air Arm)

Notes

These 31,500-ton ships are diesel-electric powered, with three refuelling rigs. They have a cargo capacity of 16,900 tonnes (Fuel) and 915 tonnes (Dry Stores). They have a large one spot flight deck, hangar and maintenance facilities capable of supporting two Merlin helicopters. They have spent extended periods in the Caribbean conducting successful counter-narcotics operations with an embarked RN helicopter. In July 2016 WAVE KNIGHT relieved the offshore patrol vessel HMS MERSEY on Caribbean patrol duties. Towards the end of 2016 WAVE RULER was operating in support of Flag Officer Sea Training and provided a flight deck for 824 NAS Merlin flying training.

RFA Tidespring

FLEET TANKERS
TIDE CLASS

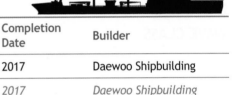

Ship	Pennant Number	Completion Date	Builder
TIDESPRING	A136	2017	Daewoo Shipbuilding
TIDERACE	*A137*	*2017*	*Daewoo Shipbuilding*
TIDESURGE	*A138*	*2018*	*Daewoo Shipbuilding*
TIDEFORCE	*A139*	*2018*	*Daewoo Shipbuilding*

Displacement 37,000 tons (FL) Dimensions 200.9m x 28.6m x 10m Machinery 2 Wärtsilä diesels, 20,394 hp; 2 shafts Speed 14.5 knots Armament fitted for 2 x Phalanx; 2 x 30mm Aircraft 1 Merlin or Wildcat Complement 63 (plus 26 spare berths)

Notes

A derivative of BMT Defence Services' AEGIR-26 design, they are double-hulled to reduce or prevent oil being lost by damage to the outer hull. Replenishment facilities comprise three abeam RAS(L) stations (two sited starboard and one to port) for diesel oil, aviation fuel and fresh water; solid RAS reception up to 2 tonnes; and vertical replenishment using an embarked helicopter (the design features a flight deck sized for a Merlin, a maintenance hangar, and an in-flight refuelling capability). Provision is also made for the future fit of a stern fuel delivery reel. The first ship is due to be delivered in 2017 for fitting of sensitive equipment at A&P Falmouth. All four are scheduled to enter service by 2018.

RFA Black Rover

SMALL FLEET TANKERS
ROVER CLASS

Ship	Pennant Number	Completion Date	Builder
GOLD ROVER	A271	1974	Swan Hunter
BLACK ROVER	A273	1974	Swan Hunter

Displacement 11,522 tons Dimensions 141m x 19m x 7m Machinery 2 SEMT-Pielstick 16 PA 4 diesels; 1 shaft; 1 bow thruster Speed 18 knots Armament 2 - 20mm guns Complement 49/54

Notes

Small Fleet Tankers designed to supply warships with fresh water, dry cargo and refrigerated provisions, as well as a range of fuels and lubricants. Helicopter deck, but no hangar. Have been employed in recent years mainly as support for HM Ships operating around the Falkland Islands and as the FOST station tanker. Now over 40 years old, GOLD ROVER sailed to the South Atlantic for her final deployment in September 2014. She was scheduled to return in 2016 to decommission, but will now remain deployed until sometime in 2017. BLACK ROVER was scheduled to conduct a further deployment in 2016 prior to decommissioning in 2017, but she remains laid up at Birkenhead and is now unlikely to return to service.

The MoD also has the commercial tanker MAERSK RAPIER under charter which supplies fuel to the naval facilities in the UK and abroad. The MoD charters the vessel to commercial companies when it is not in use for their own requirements. The tanker MT CUMBRIAN FISHER has also been occasionally chartered for moving fuel products between the UK and the Falkland Islands.

RFA Fort Rosalie

STORES VESSELS
FORT CLASS I

Ship	Pennant Number	Completion Date	Builder
FORT ROSALIE	A385	1978	Scott Lithgow
FORT AUSTIN	A386	1979	Scott Lithgow

Displacement 23,384 tons Dimensions 183m x 24m x 9m Machinery 1 Sulzer 8-cylinder RND90 diesel, 22,300 hp; 1 shaft; 2 bow thrusters Armament 2 x Vulcan Phalanx Speed 20 knots Complement 201, (120 RFA, 36 MoD Civilians & 45 Fleet Air Arm)

Notes

Full hangar and maintenance facilities are provided and up to four Sea King or Lynx helicopters can be carried for both the transfer of stores and anti-submarine protection of a group of ships (Note: these ships are not cleared to operate Merlin). Both ships can be armed with 4 - 20mm guns. FORT ROSALIE returned to the fleet in 2016 following a refit at Birkenhead. FORT AUSTIN arrived at Birkenhead in 2015 following her Gulf deployment where she remains laid up awaiting refit. FORT AUSTIN is scheduled to decommission in 2021 and FORT ROSALIE in 2022.

● JOHN NEWTH

REPLENISHMENT SHIPS
FORT CLASS II

Ship	Pennant Number	Completion Date	Builder
FORT VICTORIA	A387	1992	Harland & Wolff

Displacement 35,500 tons **Dimensions** 204m x 30m x 9m **Machinery** 2 Crossley-Pielstick V-16 diesels, 23,904 hp; 2 shafts **Speed** 20 knots **Armament** 4 x 30mm guns, 2 x Phalanx CIWS, Sea Wolf Missile System (Fitted for but not with) **Complement** 100 (RFA), 24 MoD Civilians, 32 RN and up to 122 Fleet Air Arm

Notes

A "One stop" replenishment ship with the widest range of armaments, fuel and spares carried. Can operate up to 5 Lynx or 3 Merlin Helicopters (more in a ferry role) with full maintenance facilities onboard. Medical facilities were upgraded with a 12 bed surgical capability. Under current plans she is to remain in service until 2019. In 2015 she deployed to the Gulf region and Indian Ocean in support of the anti piracy, anti smuggling and anti trafficking activities of the Combined Maritime Force, based in Bahrain. In March 2016, the ship was directed to head into the Mediterranean and act as the Command Platform for the UK contingent in support of a NATO Task Group monitoring the migrant crisis.

RFA Mounts Bay

LANDING SHIP DOCK (AUXILIARY) BAY CLASS

Ship	Pennant Number	Completion Date	Builder
LYME BAY	L3007	2007	Swan Hunter
MOUNTS BAY	L3008	2006	BAe Systems
CARDIGAN BAY	L3009	2007	BAe Systems

Displacement 16,190 tonnes Dimensions 176.6m x 26.4m x 5.1m Machinery Diesel-electric; 2 Wärtsilä 8L26 DG, 6,000 hp (4.5 MW); 2 × Wärtsilä 12V26 DG, 9,000 hp (6.7 MW); 2 azimuthing thrusters; 1 bow thruster Speed 18 knots Armament 2 x Vulcan Phalanx in some Complement 60

Notes

The dock is capable of operating LCU 10s and they carry two LCVP Mk5s. They can offload at sea, over the horizon. In addition to their war fighting role they could be well suited to disaster relief and other humanitarian missions. In 2016 MOUNTS BAY was deployed to both the Aegean and Eastern Mediterranean in support of Operation Sophia, focused on tackling human smugglers and arms traffickers. She also took part in the Joint Expeditionary Force (Maritime) 2016 deployment, taking part in a number of serials in the Adriatic. RFA CARDIGAN BAY, which had been deployed to the Gulf as the afloat forward support base ship for the RNs deployed minesweepers since 2013, returned to the UK in July 2016, having been relieved in the role by her sister LYME BAY. Following her return CARDIGAN BAY was scheduled to undergo five months of repair, maintenance and upgrades, at A&P Falmouth, before returning to service.

RFA Argus

PRIMARY CASUALTY RECEIVING SHIP/ AVIATION TRAINING SHIP

Ship	Pennant Number	Completion Date	Builder
ARGUS	A135	1981	Cantieri Navali Breda

Displacement 28,481 tons (Full Load) Dimensions 175m x 30m x 8m Machinery 2 Lindholmen Pielstick 18 PC2.5V diesels, 23,400 hp; 2 shafts; 1 bow thruster Speed 18 knots Armament 4 x 30mm, 2 x 20mm Aircraft up to 6 Merlin Complement 254 (inc 137 FAA)

Notes

The former MV CONTENDER BEZANT was purchased in 1984 and rebuilt at Harland and Wolff, Belfast, from 1984-87 to operate as an Aviation Training Ship. She undertook a rapid conversion in October 1990 to become a Primary Casualty Receiving Ship (PCRS) for service in the Gulf. These facilities were upgraded and made permanent during 2001. In 2009 the ship underwent a Service Life Extension Programme at Falmouth to switch her primary role to that of PCRS with a secondary aviation training role. The construction of new casualty access lifts together with a new deckhouse aft of the superstructure has reduced helicopter capability by one landing spot. The ship has facilities for undertaking 3 major operations simultaneously, intensive care, high dependency and general wards for up to 100 patients. It also has a dentistry operating theatre, CT scanner and X-ray units. The care facility operates with a staff of up to 250 doctors, nurses and support staff. The ship is scheduled to remain in service until 2020 although, to date, there appears to be no planned replacement.

MV Eddystone

STRATEGIC SEALIFT RO-RO VESSELS
POINT CLASS

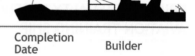

Ship	Pennant Number	Completion Date	Builder
HURST POINT		2002	Flensburger
HARTLAND POINT		2002	Harland & Wolff
EDDYSTONE		2002	Flensburger
ANVIL POINT		2003	Harland & Wolff

Displacement 10,000 tonnes, 13,300 tonnes (FL) **Dimensions** 193m x 26m x 6.6m
Machinery 2 MaK 94M43 diesels, 21,700 hp; 2 shafts; 2 CP propellors; 1 bow thruster
Speed 18 knots **Complement** 38

Notes

Foreland Shipping Limited operated 6 Ro-Ro vessels built at yards in the UK and Germany under a PFI deal which was signed with the MoD on 27 June 2002 and runs until 31 December 2024. While the current main focus is on transporting equipment to and from the Middle East/Gulf in support of military activities in Afghanistan, the vessels also make regular voyages to the Falkland Islands and to Canada and Norway in support of training exercises. The ships are all named after English lighthouses. The ships come under the operational umbrella of Defence Supply Chain Operation and Movements (DSCOM), part of the Defence Logistics Organisation. In 2012 the requirement was reduced from six to four ships. BEACHY HEAD and LONGSTONE were subsequently sold. The former was renamed WILLIAMSBORG and is operated under the Maltese flag. The latter has been operating a Ro-Ro service in Australian waters between Burnie and Melbourne.

RFA FORT VICTORIA refuelling HMAS PERTH

Commonwealth of Australia

RFA LYME BAY

US Navy

SERCO MARINE SERVICES

The tugs SD ADEPT and SD CAREFUL escort the nuclear-powered submarine HMS TORBAY in Plymouth Sound. The Fast Fleet Tanker RFA WAVE RULER can be seen in the background. (Ray Wergan)

In December 2007 the MoD signed a £1 billion Private Finance Initiative (PFI) contract with Serco Denholm Marine Services Limited for the Future Provision of Marine Services (FPMS) over the following 15 years. In 2009 Serco bought out Denholm's share and the SD funnel logos have been replaced by a prominent Serco logo on the superstructure.

Marine services embrace a wide range of waterborne and associated support activities, both in and out of port, at Portsmouth, Devonport and on the Clyde, as well as maintenance of UK and overseas moorings and navigational marks and support of a range of military operations and training.

In-port services include the provision of berthing and towage activities within the three naval bases; passenger transportation, including pilot transfers and the transportation of stores, including liquids and munitions. The recovery and disposal of waste from ships and spillage prevention and clean-up also fall within their tasking. There is also a requirement for substantial out-of-port operations. Diving training, minelaying exercises, torpedo recovery, boarding training and target towing duties are also undertaken.

The Briggs Group has been sub-contracted to assist with buoys and mooring support work. Shore based work to support these moorings and navigation buoys, have been relocated from Pembroke Dock to Burntisland on the Firth of Forth.

SHIPS OF SERCO MARINE SERVICES

Ship	Page	Ship	Page
SD ADEPT	65	SD MOORFOWL	83
SD ANGELINE	85	SD MOORHEN	83
SD BOUNTIFUL	64	SD NAVIGATOR	84
SD BOVISAND	74	SD NETLEY	75
SD CAREFUL	65	SD NEWHAVEN	75
SD CATHERINE	69	SD NORTHERN RIVER	82
SD CAWSAND	74	SD NORTON	78
SD CHRISTINA	67	SD NUTBOURNE	75
SD CLYDE RACER	86	SD OBAN	77
SD CLYDE SPIRIT	87	SD OCEANSPRAY	81
SD DEBORAH	67	SD OILMAN	81
SD DEPENDABLE	64	SD OMAGH	77
SD EILEEN	67	SD ORONSAY	77
SD EMILY	69	SD PADSTOW	76
SD ENGINEER	84	SD POWERFUL	65
SD EVA	79	SD RAASAY	84
SD FAITHFUL	65	SD RELIABLE	64
SD FLORENCE	68	SD RESOURCEFUL	64
SD FORCEFUL	65	SD SOLENT RACER	86
SD FRANCES	68	SD SOLENT SPIRIT	87
SD GENEVIEVE	68	SD SUZANNE	67
SD HELEN	68	SD TAMAR RACER	86
SD HERCULES	66	SD TAMAR SPIRIT	87
SD IMPETUS	61	SD TEESDALE	81
SD IMPULSE	61	SD TEMPEST	62
SD INDEPENDENT	63	SD TILLY	70
SD INDULGENT	63	SD VICTORIA	71
SD INSPECTOR	84	SD WARDEN	72
SD JUPITER	66	SD WATERPRESS	81
SD KYLE OF LOCHALSH	73		
SD MARS	66	Briggs Sub-Contract	
SD MELTON	80		
SD MENAI	80	CAMERON	88
SD MEON	80	KINGDOM OF FIFE	88

SD Impulse

TUGS

IMPULSE CLASS

Ship	Completion Date	Builder
SD IMPULSE	1993	R. Dunston
SD IMPETUS	1993	R. Dunston

G.R.T. 400 tons approx **Dimensions** 33m x 10m x 4m **Machinery** 2 WH Allen diesels; 3,400 hp; 2 Azimuth thrusters; 1 bow thruster **Speed** 12 knots **Complement** 5

Notes

Completed in 1993 specifically to serve as berthing tugs for the Trident Class submarines at Faslane. To be retained in service until 2022.

SD Tempest

ART 8032 CLASS

Ship	Completion Date	Builder
SD TEMPEST	2017	Damen, Gdansk

G.R.T. 495 tons **Dimensions** 32.9m x 12.6m x 6.5m **Machinery** 3 Caterpillar 3512C diesels, 5,295 kW; 3 Schottel SRP 1215 CP propellors **Speed** 13 knots **Complement** 4

Notes

Ordered in February 2016 her primary role in Portsmouth will be to support the Queen Elizabeth carriers although she will undertake other harbour work. She was launched in Gdansk on 14 September 2016 and scheduled for delivery on 29 January 2017. Equipped with a double drum render/recovery aft winch. Fitted with a foldable mast to allow her to operate under the flightdeck overhangs.

SD Independent

ASD 2509 CLASS

Ship	Completion Date	Builder
SD INDEPENDENT	2009	Damen, Gorinchem
SD INDULGENT	2009	Damen, Gorinchem

G.R.T. 345 tons approx Dimensions 26.09m x 9.44m x 4.3m Machinery 2 Caterpillar diesels; 3,500 hp; 2 RR thrusters; 1 bow thruster Speed 13 knots Complement 4

Notes

Azimuth Stern Drive (ASD) tugs. Designed for Coastal and Harbour towage, specifically modified for making cold moves within the Naval Bases. Both are based at Portsmouth.

SD Bountiful (SD Suzanne to port)

ATD 2909 CLASS

Ship	Completion Date	Builder
SD RELIABLE	2009	Damen, Stellendam
SD BOUNTIFUL	2010	Damen, Stellendam
SD RESOURCEFUL	2010	Damen, Stellendam
SD DEPENDABLE	2010	Damen, Stellendam

G.R.T. 271 tons Dimensions 29.14m x 9.98m x 4.8m Machinery 2 Caterpillar diesels; 4,025 hp; 2 RR thrusters Speed 13.1 knots Complement 4 (Portsmouth); 5 (Clyde)

Notes

Azimuthing Tractor Drive (ATD) tugs. SD BOUNTIFUL is based at Portsmouth. SD RESOURCEFUL, SD RELIABLE and SD DEPENDABLE are based on the Clyde. Designed for Coastal and Harbour towage, specifically modified for making cold moves within the Naval Bases. Two double drum towing winches are fitted, along with extensive underwater fendering, fire fighting equipment and facilities for passenger and stores transportation.

SD Adept

TWIN UNIT TRACTOR TUGS

Ship	Completion Date	Builder
SD ADEPT	1980	R. Dunston
SD CAREFUL	1982	R. Dunston
SD FAITHFUL	1985	R. Dunston
SD FORCEFUL	1985	R. Dunston
SD POWERFUL	1985	R. Dunston

G.R.T. 384 tons Dimensions 38.8m x 9.42m x 4m Machinery 2 Ruston diesels; 2,575 hp; 2 Voith-Schneider propellors Speed 12 knots Complement 5

Notes

The principal harbour tugs in naval service. Some are to undergo a service life extension programme. All based at Devonport except SD POWERFUL, which is based at Portsmouth. Intention is to return SD POWERFUL to Devonport once SD TEMPEST enters service (page 62).

SD Jupiter

STAN TUG 2608 CLASS

Ship	Completion Date	Builder
SD HERCULES	2009	Damen, Gorinchem
SD JUPITER	2009	Damen, Gorinchem
SD MARS	2009	Damen, Gorinchem

G.R.T. 133.92 tons **Dimensions** 26.61m x 8.44m x 4.05m **Machinery** 2 Caterpillar diesels; 2,200 hp; 2 Van de Giessen nozzles **Speed** 12 knots **Complement** 4 (6 max)

Notes

A conventional Twin Screw Tug design. SD HERCULES and SD MARS are based at Devonport. SD JUPITER is based on the Clyde. All can be used to handle submarine mounted Towed Arrays.

SD Deborah

ASD 2009 CLASS

Ship	Completion Date	Builder
SD CHRISTINA	2010	Damen, Gdynia
SD DEBORAH	2010	Damen, Gdynia
SD EILEEN	2010	Damen, Gdynia
SD SUZANNE	2010	Damen, Gdynia

G.R.T. 120.74 tons Dimensions 21.2m x 9.4m x 3.6m Machinery 2 Caterpillar diesels; 2,000 hp; 2 RR thrusters Speed 11 knots Complement 3

Notes

Azimuth Stern Drive tugs derived from the successful Damen ASD 2411 shiphandling tug. Winches fore and aft, together with a bow thruster, make these tugs suitable for handling smaller surface ship, barge work and assisting with submarine movements. SD DEBORAH and SD EILEEN are based at Devonport, SD CHRISTINA and SD SUZANNE at Portsmouth.

SD Helen

FELICITY CLASS

Ship	Completion Date	Builder
SD FLORENCE	1980	R. Dunston
SD FRANCES	1980	R. Dunston
SD GENEVIEVE	1980	R. Dunston
SD HELEN	1974	R. Dunston

G.R.T. 88.96 tons Dimensions 22.0m x 6.4m x 2.6m Machinery 1 Mirrlees-Blackstone diesel; 615 hp; 1 Voith-Schneider CP propellor Speed 10 knots Complement 4

Notes

Water Tractors used for the movement of small barges and equipment. SD FRANCES and SD FLORENCE based at Devonport, with the other pair at Portsmouth.

SD Catherine

PUSHY CAT 1204

Ship	Completion Date	Builder
SD CATHERINE	2008	Damen, Gorinchem
SD EMILY	2008	Damen, Gorinchem

G.R.T. 29.4 tons Dimensions 12.3m x 4.13m x 1.55m Machinery 1 Caterpillar diesel; 165 hp; 1 shaft Speed 8 knots Complement 2

Notes

Powered by a single Caterpillar 3056 TA diesel driving a single screw. A propulsion nozzle is fitted, and twin rudders to give a 2.1 tons bollard pull. SD CATHERINE is based at Portsmouth, SD EMILY at Devonport. General line runner and harbour workboat.

SD Tilly

STAN TUG 1405

Ship	Completion Date	Builder
SD TILLY	2009	Damen, Gorinchem

G.R.T. 45 tons **Dimensions** 14.55m x 4.98m x 1.8m **Machinery** 2 Caterpillar diesels; 600 hp; 2 Van de Giessen nozzles **Speed** 9 knots **Complement** 3

Notes

A general purpose inshore and harbour tug based at Devonport. A twin screw version of the Pushy Cat 1204. Slightly larger with a bow thruster and also developing 8 tonnes bollard pull. Line handler, general workboat and ideal for moving small barges.

SD Victoria

WORLDWIDE SUPPORT VESSEL

Ship	Completion Date	Builder
SD VICTORIA	2010	Damen, Galatz

G.R.T. 3,522 tons Dimensions 83m x 16m x 4.5m Machinery 2 Caterpillar diesels; 4,000 hp; 2 shafts; CP propellors; 1 bow thruster Speed 14 knots Complement 16 (Accommodation for 72)

Notes

Powered by two Caterpillar 3516B diesels driving two shafts with controllable pitch propellors SD VICTORIA is designed to support training operations around the world. Capable of transporting both personnel and equipment and supporting diving operations. She is equipped with classrooms, briefing rooms and operations rooms in addition to workshop facilities. There is provision to carry and operate RIBs and there is a helicopter winching deck. Note Fast Interceptor Craft under covers on the quarterdeck. Based at Greenock but spends time in Devonport loading for her various customers.

SD Warden

TRIALS VESSEL

Ship	Completion Date	Builder
SD WARDEN	1989	Richards

Displacement 626 tons **Dimensions** 48m x 10m x 4m **Machinery** 2 Ruston diesels; 4,000 hp; 2 shafts; CP propellors **Speed** 15 knots **Complement** 11

Notes

Built as a Range Maintenance Vessel but now based at Kyle of Lochalsh and operated in support of British Underwater Test and Evaluation Centre (BUTEC). Also operates as a Remotely Operated Vehicle (ROV) platform. A replacement ROV has been installed and set to work to replace the older system. To remain in service until 2022.

SD Kyle of Lochalsh

TRIALS VESSEL

Ship	Completion Date	Builder
SD KYLE OF LOCHALSH	1997	Abel, Bristol

Displacement 120 tons Dimensions 24.35m x 9m x 3.45m Machinery 2 Caterpillar diesels; 2,992 hp; 2 shafts Speed 10.5 knots Complement 4

Notes

The former twin screw tug MCS LENIE which has now been purchased from Maritime Craft Services (Clyde) Ltd by Serco Marine Services. She is used to support trials and operations at Kyle of Lochalsh.

SD Bovisand

TENDERS
STORM CLASS

Ship	Completion Date	Builder
SD BOVISAND	1997	FBM (Cowes)
SD CAWSAND	1997	FBM (Cowes)

G.R.T 225 tonnes Dimensions 23m x 11m x 2m Machinery 2 Caterpillar diesels; 1,224 hp; 2 shafts Speed 15 knots Complement 5

Notes

These craft are used in support of Flag Officer Sea Training (FOST) at Plymouth to transfer staff quickly and comfortably to and from Warships and Auxiliaries within and beyond the Plymouth breakwater in open sea conditions. These are the first vessels of a small waterplane area twin hull (SWATH) design to be ordered by the Ministry of Defence and cost £6.5 million each. Speed restrictions implemented due to wash problems generated by these vessels. To remain in service until 2022.

SD Netley

NEWHAVEN CLASS

Ship	Completion Date	Builder
SD NEWHAVEN	2000	Aluminium SB
SD NUTBOURNE	2000	Aluminium SB
SD NETLEY	2001	Aluminium SB

Tonnage 77 tonnes (45 grt) Dimensions 18.3m x 6.8m x 1.88m Machinery 2 Cummins diesels; 710 hp; 2 shafts Speed 10 knots Complement 2/3 Crew (60 passengers)

Notes

MCA Class IV Passenger Vessels acquired as replacements for Fleet tenders. Employed on general passenger duties within the port area. To remain in service until 2022. SD NETLEY and SD NUTBOURNE are based at Portsmouth, SD NEWHAVEN is based at Devonport and operates in support of Flag Officer Sea Training (FOST). Has undergone modifications to strengthen her forward bollard and add transfer wings to enable underway personnel transfers with some classes of vessel undertaking sea training. Utilised if SD CAWSAND, SD BOVISAND or SD OBAN are out of service or unavailable.

SD Padstow

PADSTOW CLASS

Ship	Completion Date	Builder
SD PADSTOW	2000	Aluminium SB

Tonnage 77 tonnes (45 grt) Dimensions 18.3m x 6.8m x 1.88m Machinery 2 Cummins diesels; 710 hp; 2 shafts Speed 10 knots Complement 2/3 Crew (60 passengers)

Notes

MCA Class IV, VI and VIA Passenger Vessel based at Devonport. Used on liberty runs in Plymouth Sound and the Harbour as well as occasionally supporting FOST. Has undergone similar modifications as SD NEWHAVEN (previous page) in order to conduct underway personnel transfers. To remain in service until 2022.

SD Oronsay

OBAN CLASS

Ship	Completion Date	Builder
SD OBAN	2000	McTay Marine
SD ORONSAY	2000	McTay Marine
SD OMAGH	2000	McTay Marine

G.R.T 199 tons Dimensions 27.7m x 7.30m x 3.75m Machinery 2 Cummins diesels; 1,050 hp; 2 Kort-nozzles Speed 10 knots Complement 4 Crew (60 passengers)

Notes

MCA Class IIA Passenger Vessels which replaced Fleet tenders in 2001. SD OBAN was transferred to Devonport in 2003 and is now primarily used to support FOST staff. SD ORONSAY and SD OMAGH employed on general passenger duties on the Clyde and are additionally classified as Cargo Ship VIII(A). To remain in service until 2022.

SD Norton

PERSONNEL FERRY

Ship	Completion Date	Builder
SD NORTON	1989	FBM Marine

G.R.T 21 tons **Dimensions** 15.8m x 5.5m x 1.5m **Machinery** 2 Mermaid Turbo diesels; 280 hp; 2 shafts **Speed** 13 knots **Complement** 2

Notes

The single FBM catamaran, 8837, operated at Portsmouth. Can carry 30 passengers or 2 tons of stores. Was a prototype catamaran designed to replace older Harbour Launches but no more were ordered.

SD Eva

PERSONNEL FERRY

Ship	Completion Date	Builder
SD EVA	2009	Damen

G.R.T 168 tons Dimensions 33.21m x 7.4m x 3.3m Machinery 2 Caterpillar diesels; 2,800 hp; 2 shafts Speed 23.4 knots Complement 4-6 (plus 34 passengers)

Notes

Operated on the Clyde as a Fast Crew Transport. The Axe Bow design allows the vessel to effectively cut through waves with minimal movement of the vessel. The vessel is the first of its type in the UK to be operated under the International Code of Safety for High Speed Craft (HSC Code). She is no longer on contract, having been released in 2016. Although still owned by Serco she is currently laid up on the Clyde.

SD Melton

FLEET TENDERS

Ship	Completion Date	Builder
SD MELTON	1981	Richard Dunston
SD MENAI	1981	Richard Dunston
SD MEON	1982	Richard Dunston

G.R.T. 117.3 tons Dimensions 24m x 6.7m x 3.05m Machinery 1 Lister Blackstone diesel; 320 hp; 1 shaft Speed 10.5 knots Complement 4 (12 passengers)

Notes

The last three survivors of a once numerous class of vessels used as Training Tenders, Passenger Ferries, or Cargo Vessels. MENAI and MEON are operated at Falmouth. MELTON is operated at Kyle of Lochalsh. A vessel replacement programme now seems unlikely and this elderly trio are expected to remain in service until 2022.

SD Teesdale

COASTAL OILER

Ship	Completion Date	Builder
SD TEESDALE	1976	Yorkshire Drydock Co.

G.R.T. 499 tons **Dimensions** 43.86m x 9.5m x 3.92m **Speed** 8 knots **Complement** 5

Notes

Formerly the oil products tanker TEESDALE H operated by John H Whitaker. Operates as a parcel tanker delivering diesel and aviation fuel and also delivering / receiving compensating water. She is self propelled by two Aquamaster thrusters.

A Diesel Lighter Barge, SD OILMAN, and a Water Lighter Barge, SD WATERPRESS, are operated on the Clyde. A further barge, a Liquid Mixed Lighter Barge, SD OCEANSPRAY, is based at Portsmouth.

● DEREK FOX

SD Northern River

MULTI-PURPOSE VESSEL

Ship	Completion Date	Builder
SD NORTHERN RIVER	1998	Myklebust (Norway)

G.R.T 3,605 tons   Dimensions 92.8m x 18.8m x 4.9m   Machinery 2 Bergen diesels; 9,598 hp; 2 shafts; CP propellors; 2 bow thrusters   Speed 14 knots   Complement 14

Notes

Bought from Deep Ocean AS (a subsidiary of Trico Marine) this Ulstein UT-745L designed Support Vessel entered service with Serco in March 2012. She can be employed on a variety of tasking from target towing, through noise ranging to data gathering; boarding training to submarine escort. Her extensive flat work deck allows her to embark containers for passive sonar training. She can also provide nuclear emergency support as well as support to submarine emergencies. She can provide mother ship training facilities for the NATO Submarine Rescue System (NSRS), which involves the embarkation, fitting and operation of specialist ROV's, escape vessels and Transfer Under Pressure (TUP) facilities on the after deck, together with the embarkation of up to 40 additional personnel. She can also support the Submarine Parachute Assistance Group.

SD Moorhen

DIVING SUPPORT VESSELS
MOOR CLASS

Ship	Completion Date	Builder
SD MOORFOWL	1989	McTay Marine
SD MOORHEN	1989	McTay Marine

Displacement 518 tons Dimensions 32m x 11m x 2m Machinery 2 Cummins diesels; 796 hp; 2 Aquamasters; 1 bow thruster Speed 8 knots Complement 10

Notes

Designed as a powered mooring lighter for use within sheltered coastal waters the lifting horns have been removed from the bows of both vessels when they were converted to Diving Support Vessels. They are used by the Defence Diving School for diving training in the Kyle of Lochalsh. To remain in service until 2022.

SD Navigator

MULTICAT 2510 CLASS

Ship	Completion Date	Builder
SD NAVIGATOR	2009	Damen, Hardinxveld
SD RAASAY	2010	Damen, Hardinxveld

G.R.T 150.27 tonnes Dimensions 26.3m x 10.64m x 2.55m Machinery 2 Caterpillar diesels; 957 hp; 2 shafts Speed 8 knots Complement 3 (plus up to 12 additional personnel)

Notes

SD NAVIGATOR is equipped for buoy handling with a single 9 ton capacity crane. She is capable of supporting diving operations. SD RAASAY is based at the Kyle of Lochalsh. She is fitted with two cranes for torpedo recovery and support diving training. SD NAVIGATOR is managed from Portsmouth, but operates between Devonport and Portsmouth. Two similar vessels, SD INSPECTOR (ex-DMS EAGLE) and SD ENGINEER operate from Portsmouth and Devonport respectively.

SD Angeline

MULTICAT 2613S CLASS

Ship	Completion Date	Builder
SD ANGELINE	2015	Damen, Gorinchem

G.R.T 200 tonnes Dimensions 26.25m x 13m x 3.7m Machinery 2 Caterpillar C32 TTA diesels; 2 fixed pitch propellors; bow thruster Speed 10.1 knots Complement Accommodation for 8 persons, consisting of four double crew cabins

Notes

Her total power output is 2,850 kW with a bollard pull of 45 tons. The crane has a capacity of 15 tm. Ordered April 2014 Accepted by the MoD in April 2015 although there are still operational trials to take place. Built at the request of the MoD to provide support in Faslane Naval Base primarily to submarines, but can undertake other naval base work.

SD Tamar Racer

STAN TENDER 1505 CLASS

Ship	Completion Date	Builder
SD CLYDE RACER	2008	Damen, Gorinchem
SD SOLENT RACER	2008	Damen, Gorinchem
SD TAMAR RACER	2008	Damen, Gorinchem

G.R.T 25.19 tonnes Dimensions 16m x 4.85m x 1.25m Machinery 2 Caterpillar diesels; 1,100 hp; 2 shafts Speed 20 knots Complement 3 (+ 10 Passengers)

Notes ·

Of aluminium construction these boats are employed on transfer of pilots, port security operations and passenger and VIP transportation.

SD Solent Spirit

STAN TENDER 1905 CLASS

Ship	Completion Date	Builder
SD CLYDE SPIRIT	2008	Damen, Gorinchem
SD SOLENT SPIRIT	2008	Damen, Gorinchem
SD TAMAR SPIRIT	2008	Damen, Gorinchem

G.R.T 43.3 tonnes Dimensions 18.91m x 5.06m x 1.65m Machinery 2 Caterpillar diesels; 2,200 hp; 2 shafts Speed 21.7 knots Complement 3 (+ 10 passengers)

Notes

Steel hull with aluminium superstructure. Special propellor tunnels are fitted to increase propulsion efficiency and to reduce vibration and noise levels. These vessels are able to operate safely and keep good performance in wind speeds up to Force 6 and wave heights of 2 metres. Employed on transfer of pilots, VIPs and personnel.

Kingdom of Fife

ANCHOR HANDLING TUG

Ship	Completion Date	Builder
KINGDOM OF FIFE	2008	Damen, Galatz

Displacement 1,459 tons Dimensions 61.2m x 13.5m x 4.75m Machinery 2 Caterpillar diesels, 2,720 hp each; 1 shaft; bow thruster Speed 13.7 knots Complement 18

Notes

Briggs Marine won a £100m contract from Serco to support navigation buoy maintenance and mooring support for the Royal Navy for 15 years. During the contract period, Briggs Marine provide support for over 350 moorings, navigation buoys and targets for the RN all around the UK coast, as well as Cyprus, Gibraltar and the Falkland Islands. KINGDOM OF FIFE was delivered in May 2008 and supports the existing Briggs Marine shallow draught and heavy lift craft CAMERON in servicing the contract and can be equipped with a decompression chamber with support from the Serco dive team.

● JOHN CRAE

AIRCREW TRAINING VESSELS

Ship	Comp Date	Builder	Base Port
SMIT DEE	2003	BES Rosyth	Buckie
SMIT DART	2003	BES Rosyth	Plymouth
SMIT DON	2003	BES Rosyth	Blyth
SMIT YARE	2003	FBMA Cebu	Great Yarmouth
SMIT SPEY	2003	FBMA Cebu	Plymouth

G.R.T. 95.86 GRT **Dimensions** 27.6m x 6.6m x 1.5m **Machinery** 2 Cummins diesels; 1,400 hp; 2 shafts; 1 centreline waterjet; 305hp **Speed** 21 knots **Complement** 6

Notes

The service for Marine Support to Range Safety and Aircrew Training is provided by SMIT International (Scotland) Ltd and runs until April 2018. These vessels provide support to aircrew training through serials such as sea survival drills, various helicopter exercises, target towing and other general marine support tasks. They also participate in Navy Command sea training serials, particularly boarding exercises and force protection exercises involving fast attack craft scenarios. SMIT DART completed as a passenger vessel with a larger superstructure. SMIT TOWY and the smaller SMIT TAMAR will no longer be used to deliver the service after March 2017.

Smit Cerne

RANGE SAFETY VESSELS

Ship	Comp Date	Builder
SMIT STOUR	2003	Maritime Partners Norway
SMIT ROTHER	2003	Maritime Partners Norway
SMIT ROMNEY	2003	Maritime Partners Norway
SMIT CERNE	2003	Maritime Partners Norway
SMIT FROME	2003	Maritime Partners Norway
SMIT MERRION	2003	Maritime Partners Norway
SMIT PENALLY	2003	Maritime Partners Norway
SMIT WEY	2003	Maritime Partners Norway
SMIT NEYLAND	2003	Maritime Partners Norway

G.R.T. 7.0 GRT Dimensions 12.3m x 2.83m x 0.89m Machinery 2 Volvo Penta diesels; 680 hp; 2 Hamilton waterjets Speed 35 knots Complement 2

Notes

A class of 12 metre Fast Patrol Craft which provide a range safety service to 7 land based ranges across the UK. They also participate in Navy Command Sea Training serials including participation in Fast Attack Craft scenarios.

AWB Sirocco

ARMY VESSELS
WORK BOATS

Vessel	Pennant Number	Completion Date	Builder
STORM	WB41	2008	Warbreck Eng.
DIABLO	WB42	2008	Warbreck Eng.
MISTRAL	WB43	2008	Warbreck Eng.
SIROCCO	WB44	2008	Warbreck Eng.

Displacement 48 tonnes Dimensions 14.75m x 4.30m Machinery 2 John Deere Diesels; 402 hp; 2 shafts Speed 10 knots Complement 4

Notes

Part of the Army's strategic port operations in Southampton, but can be transported by a 'mother ship' to other ports and places like Iraq. Are often used as tugs for mex-eflotes, positioning other pontoon equipment and for handling flexible pipelines. They have a firefighting capability. The Army also operate a number of smaller Combat Support Boats. Built by RTK Marine/VT Halmatic (now BAE) these are fast and rugged small craft, 8.8m long with a twin Hamilton waterjet propulsion system powered by twin 210hp diesel engines.

HMC Seeker

BORDER FORCE
STAN PATROL 4207 CLASS

Vessel	Pennant Number	Completion Date	Builder
SEARCHER	-	2002	Damen
SEEKER	-	2001	Damen
VALIANT	-	2004	Damen
VIGILANT	-	2003	Damen

Displacement 238 GRT Dimensions 42.8m x 7.11m x 2.52m Machinery 2 Caterpillar 3516 diesels, 2 shafts; CP propellors; bow thruster Speed 26+ knots
Complement 12

Notes
These vessels are able to remain at sea for extended periods and in heavy weather conditions. They operate 24 hours a day, 365 days per year, through the employment of dual crews. There are ten crews for the five Border Force cutters comprising 120 seagoing staff, working two weeks on and two weeks off. Cutters are mostly deployed on a risk-led or intelligence-led basis detecting prohibited and restricted goods, boarding and searching ships and providing a law enforcement presence in remote and inaccessible areas. Vessels are prefixed HMC for Her Majesty's Cutter. All five cutters are based at Portsmouth.

HMC Protector

TELKKÄ CLASS

Vessel	Pennant Number	Completion Date	Builder
PROTECTOR	-	2002	UKI Workboat

Displacement 400 tonnes Dimensions 49.7m x 7.5m x 3.9m Machinery 2 Wärtsilä 12V 200 diesels, 7,240 hp; 2 shafts; CP propellor; bow and stern thrusters Speed 22 knots Complement 12

Notes

Acquired in 2013 she is the former Finnish Border Agency vessel TAVI. Twice deployed to the Mediterranean as part of Operation Triton, led by Frontex, the EU's external border control agency. There she conducted search and rescue operations and helped in tackling the criminal gangs that are responsible for illegal attempts to move large numbers of migrants across the Mediterranean.

Eagle

DELTA ARRC 190 CLASS

Vessel	Pennant Number	Completion Date	Builder
ex-ERIK	ARRC-1	2006	Delta ARRC, Stockport
ex-SCOTT	ARRC-2	2006	Delta ARRC, Stockport
ex-PAUL	ARRC-3	2006	Delta ARRC, Stockport
ex-IAIN	ARRC-4	2006	Delta ARRC, Stockport
ex-EUAN	ARRC-5	2006	Delta ARRC, Stockport
ex-JAMES	ARRC-6	2006	Delta ARRC, Stockport
ex-ALISTAIR	ARRC-7	2006	Delta ARRC, Stockport
ex-DAVID	ARRC-8	2006	Delta ARRC, Stockport

Displacement 29 GRT Dimensions 18.8m x 4m x 0.9m Machinery 2 Caterpillar diesels, 1,000 hp; 2 Hamilton waterjets Speed 35 knots Complement ..

Notes

The rescue of migrants attempting to cross the English Channel in May highlighted the lack of Border Force vessels patrolling the UK coastline. To boost numbers eight ex BP Project Jigsaw rescue craft, built by Delta Power and the largest RiBs in the world, were acquired by Border Force. Four are now in service with the remaining four entering service within 18 months. Very little information has been released but names identified to date include EAGLE and NIMROD.

AIRCRAFT

Until 2006 the Royal Navy operated designated air groups on its aircraft carriers, each comprising a number of naval air squadrons that embarked whenever the ship was at sea to form a single, flexible entity. However, since the premature withdrawal of the Sea Harrier from service different methods have evolved to meet the increasingly joint nature of command and control for deployed operations required by a succession of Governments. Navy, Army and Air Force units are now embarked in what are known as Tailored Air Groups or TAGs. Different units, including the naval air squadrons in a much-reduced Fleet Air Arm, now come under four different administrative commands for their direction and management; these are Navy Command, Joint Force Lightning, Joint Helicopter Command and the UK Military Flying Training System. The latter organisation trains all British aircrew and is run under contract to the Ministry of Defence (MoD) by a consortium known as 'Ascent'.

Navy Command, based at Whale Island in Portsmouth, directs and manages the Royal Navy in accordance with national legislation and the requirements of the MOD. Within its structure there are 'type commanders' responsible for individual disciplines, one of which is the Fleet Air Arm. Navy Command's purpose is to provide fully trained ships, personnel, aircraft and equipment as directed by the Joint Forces Command at Northwood which commands and controls all deployed UK forces. The Table shows squadrons that can embark as part of a TAG in QUEEN ELIZABETH and PRINCE OF WALES when they enter operational service after 2020 and the helicopters that can make up a TAG in OCEAN until 2019.

The operational aircraft listed all have digital maintenance systems which are shared with partners and allies but which differ across the TAG. Thus the autonomic logistic information system, ALIS, is shared with the US armed forces and other F-35 users; the Merlin has its own different system and the Wildcat yet another one shared, in this case, with the Army Air Corps. All of them are paperless and each type has a Project Team at Abbey Wood responsible for its maintenance, support and airworthiness.

In 2017 RN and RAF personnel are serving in VMFAT-501, the squadron at MCAS Beaufort in South Carolina that is training both USMC and UK pilots and technicians to fly and maintain the F-35B Lightning II. New British F-35Bs are being delivered to Beaufort where they will form 617 Squadron which is due to move to Marham in the UK in 2018. The next British squadron to form is 809 NAS but there has been no clear indication from the MoD about when it is to achieve initial operational capability. The first unit to embark in QUEEN ELIZABETH for trials in 2018 is to be 17 Squadron, at present at Edwards Air Force base in California. Once QUEEN ELIZABETH becomes operational from 2021 it is likely that she will embark USMC F-35B and MV-22 Osprey Tilt-rotor squadrons on a regular basis alongside British units and future editions may include a list of Marine squadrons that are capable of forming part of an Allied TAG in the British carriers.

Political enthusiasm for joint forces has, thus, replaced the cohesive Fleet Air Arm, a ship-centric force once administered by a single flag officer, with a disparate group of administrative commands which use different management and logistic tools. Naval personnel have always been trained to fight as part of a ship's company. In 2017 there can be no certainty that TAG members from other Services will have the same naval training or the same easy familiarity with the sea environment. Significantly, no other Navy has adopted such a radical concept of carrier operation. Until it is tested in action against a credible naval adversary, we cannot be certain that the seismic changes of the last decade have been either a good idea or a politically-inspired failure.

David Hobbs
Consultant Editor (Naval Aviation)

AIRCRAFT & UNITS

NAVY COMMAND SQUADRONS

814 NAS	Merlin HM2	TAG/RNAS Culdrose
815 NAS	Wildcat HMA2	Flights/RNAS Yeovilton
820 NAS	Merlin HM2	TAG/RNAS Culdrose
824 NAS	Merlin HM2	Training/RNAS Culdrose
825 NAS	Wildcat HMA2	Training/RNAS Yeovilton
829 NAS	Merlin H 2	Flights/RNAS Culdrose
849 NAS	Sea King ASaC7	Flights/RNAS Culdrose
727 NAS	Tutor T1	Grading/RNAS Yeovilton
736 NAS	Hawk T1	FOST/RNAS Culdrose
FOST Flight	Dauphin 2	HMNB Devonport
RNHF	Various	RNAS Yeovilton
FNHT	Sea Vixen FAW2	RNAS Yeovilton

JOINT FORCE LIGHTNING/UNITED STATES MARINE CORPS

VMFA-501	F-35B Lightning II (training)	MCAS Beaufort - USA
17 Sqn	F-35B Lightning II	Edwards AFB - USA
617 Sqn	F-35B Lightning II (forming)	MCAS Beaufort - USA
809 NAS	F-35B Lightning II (projected)	TBA

AIRCRAFT & UNITS

JOINT HELICOPTER COMMAND

845 NAS	Merlin HC3/3i	TAG/RNAS Yeovilton
846 NAS	Merlin HC3/3i	TAG/RNAS Yeovilton
847 NAS	Wildcat AH1	TAG/RNAS Yeovilton
7 Sqn	Chinook HC4/4A/5	TAG/RAF Odiham
18 Sqn	Chinook HC4/4A/5	TAG/RAF Odiham
27 Sqn	Chinook HC4/4A/5	TAG/RAF Odiham
28(AC) Sqn	Chinook HC4/4A/5	Training/RAF Odiham
1 Regt.	Wildcat AH1	TAG/RNAS Yeovilton
3 Regt.	Apache AH1	TAG/AAC Wattisham
4 Regt.	Apache AH1	TAG/AAC Wattisham

MILITARY FLYING TRAINING SYSTEM

4(R) Sqn	Hawk T2	4 FTS/RAF Valley
72(R) Sqn	Tucano T1	1 FTS/RAF Linton-on-Ouse
703 NAS	Tutor T1	3 FTS/RAF Barkston Heath
750 NAS	Avenger T1	RNAS Culdrose
705 NAS	Squirrel HT1	RAF Shawbury

DANIEL FERRO

Leonardo Helicopters MERLIN HM2

Role Anti-submarine search and strike; maritime surveillance
Engines 3 x Rolls Royce/Turbomeca RTM 322 each developing 2,100 shp
Length 74' 10" Rotor diameter 61' Height 21' 10"
Max Weight 32,120lb Max Speed 167 knots Crew 1/2 pilots, 1 observer, 1 aircrewman
Avionics Blue Kestrel radar; Orange Reaper ESM; Folding Light Acoustic System for heli-
copters (FLASH); AQS-903 acoustic processor; Wescam MX-15 electro-optical/IR cam-
era; defensive aids including Directional Infrared Countermeasures (DIRCM), AN/AAR-
57 radar warning system, chaff and flare dispensers;
Armament Up to 4 Stingray torpedoes or Mark 11 depth charges; 1 x M3M 0.5" machine-
gun in cabin door and 1 x 7.62mm machine-gun in cabin window

Squadron Service 814, 820, 824, 829 Naval Air Squadrons

Notes
814 and 820 provide TAG detachments to OCEAN and RFAs and are preparing to form
part of the QUEEN ELIZABETH battle group. 829 NAS provides single aircraft flights to
Type 23 frigates specialising in anti-submarine operations and 824 NAS is the type's
training and tactical development unit. All are shore-based at RNAS Culdrose when not
embarked. The last of 30 Merlins upgraded from HM 1 to HM 2 standard was delivered
in 2016 and airframes are being modified during 2017 to enable them to be fitted,
optionally, with the palletised 'Cerberus' mission system under project 'Crowsnest' in
place of the anti-submarine avionics. This will enable them to be used for either A/S
or ASaC missions as required for TAG deployments and training. Up to 10 Crowsnest
sets are being planned, of which 7 are likely to be installed in Merlins operated by 849
NAS at any one time and the remainder held as a contingency reserve. The designation
to be applied to 'Crowsnest' Merlin HM 2s has yet to be announced. Unconverted HM
1s are being used as a source of spare parts.

Leonardo Helicopters WILDCAT HMA2

Roles Surface search and strike; anti-submarine strike; boarding party support
Engines 2 x LHTEC CTS 800 each developing 1,362 shp
Length 50' **Rotor diameter** 42' **Height** 12'
Max Weight 13,200lb **Max Speed** 157 knots **Crew** 1 pilot & 1 observer
Avionics Selex-Galileo Sea Spray 7400E multi-mode AESA radar; Wescam MX-15 electro-optical/IR camera; Electronic warfare system and defensive aids suite. Bowman communications system
Armament 2 x Stingray torpedoes or Mark 11 depth charges; 1 x M3M 0.5" machine-gun in cabin door. From 2020 to carry Martlet (light) and Sea Venom (heavy) air-to-surface guided weapons.

Squadron Service 815, 825 Naval Air Squadrons

Notes
825 NAS is the training and tactical development unit and 815 NAS deploys flights of 1 or 2 aircraft to destroyers, frigates that do not embark Merlins and some RFAs. Wildcat is designed around a digital avionics management system that enhances mission effectiveness and reduces aircrew workload. Its 'paperless' maintenance system is shared with the Wildcat AH 1 operated by the Joint Helicopter Command. With the Lynx HMA 8 withdrawn from service in 2017, Wildcats now fully equip these two naval air squadrons which are both shore-based at RNAS Yeovilton. The HMA 2 is to have a significant strike capability when the Martlet and Sea Venom air-to-surface guided weapons achieve initial operational capability after 2020. With the withdrawal from service of 700X NAS ScanEagle detachments in 2017, Wildcats and Merlins are the only air assets capable of deployment in destroyers, frigates and RFAs.

Leonardo Helicopters SEA KING ASaC7

Role Airborne Surveillance and Control
Engines 2 x Rolls Royce Gnome H 1400 each developing 1,600 shp
Length 54' 9" Rotor diameter 62' Height 17' 2"
Max Weight 21,400lb Max Speed 125 knots Crew 1 pilot and 2 observers
Avionics Cerberus mission system; Searchwater radar; Orange Crop ESM; Link 16;
AN/AAR-57 missile approach warning system; IR jammer; radar warning receiver; automatic chaff and flare dispenser
Armament none

Squadron Service 849 Naval Air Squadron

Notes
849 NAS operates the last 7 Sea Kings in RN service; the first production Sea King HAS 1, XV 642, flew on 7 May 1969 and the first squadron, 700S NAS, formed in July 1969. Under present plans the type is to stay in service until 2018 when it is to be replaced by 'Crowsnest' Merlins. 849 NAS is shore-based at RNAS Culdrose but has 3 Flights, named Palembang, Okinawa and Normandy after 3 of its battle honours, available for TAGs or deployments. ASaC 7s have been deployed to the Persian Gulf monitoring seafaring activity since the end of 2014 and successive detachments have completed more than 1,000 flying hours supporting the international naval effort in the region. Depending on the date set for the last airframe to be retired, the Sea King might just pass 50 years in RN service, a remarkable achievement.

BAE Systems HAWK T1

Role Threat simulation aircraft
Engine 1 x Rolls Royce Adour 151 delivering 5,200lb of thrust.
Length 40' 9" Wingspan 32' 7" Height 13' 1"
Max Weight 20,000lb Max Speed Mach 0.88 (Mach 1.2 in a dive) Crew 1 or 2 pilots
Avionics standard communications fit
Armament Can be fitted with a 30mm gun pod on a centreline pylon and one pylon under each wing capable of taking AIM-9 Sidewinder or up to 1,500lb of practice weapons

Squadron Service 736 Naval Air Squadron

Notes
736 NAS is the focal point for fixed-wing flying standards and practices within the Navy Command structure and provides continuity flying for pilots destined to be fed into the F-35B Lightning II training programme. It also provides aircraft for fighter controller and ASaC observer training plus attack simulations for FOST activities and 'Joint Warrior' exercises, effectively acting as an RN 'aggressor unit'. The aircraft are maintained by Babcock, regularly operated from both RN Air Stations Culdrose and Yeovilton and frequently deploy in support of exercises and fleet deployments. Under current plans 736 NAS' Hawk T1s are due to be withdrawn from service in 2020 although T1s operated by Air Command, including those flown by the Red Arrows display team, are expected to run on for longer. The MoD has made no statement about replacement options.

STEVE WRIGHT

Lockheed Martin F-35B LIGHTNING II

Role Strike, fighter and reconnaissance aircraft
Engine 1 X Pratt & Whitney F135-PW-600 delivering 41,000lb thrust with reheat in conventional flight; 40,650lb hover thrust with Rolls-Royce lift fan engaged and tail nozzle rotated.
Length 51' 4"   Wingspan 35'   Height 15'
Max Weight 60,000lb Max Speed Mach 1.6 Crew 1 pilot
Avionics AN/APG-81 AESA radar; AN/AAQ-40 electro-optical targeting system; AN/AAQ-37 distributed aperture system; AN/ASQ-239 'Barracuda' electronic warfare system; pilot's helmet-mounted display system; multi-function advanced data link.
Armament Current Block 2B software allows the stealthy carriage of weapons in 2 internal bays with a single ASRAAM or AMRAAM air-to-air missile plus a single 1,000lb bomb equivalent such as Paveway IV LGB in each. Block 3F software in operational aircraft delivered from 2017 will enable the additional use of 7 non-stealthy external pylons, 3 under each wing and 1 under the centreline. A total of 12,000lb of weapons or fuel tanks to be carried; inner wing pylons have 'plumbing' for 426 US gallon drop tanks.
Squadron Service VMFAT-501, 17 Squadron, 617 Squadron (forming within VMFAT-501), 809 NAS (projected to form within VMFAT-501).

Notes
The only British military aircraft to have an American rather than a British type designation, a fact that reflects the international nature of its support software. Naval and air force pilots and technicians serve in VMFAT-501 at MCAS Beaufort, South Carolina, which has one British F-35B added to its USMC aircraft and trains both American and British personnel. 617 Squadron, manned by roughly equal numbers of RN and RAF personnel, is due to reach IOC in 2019. The UK is to procure 138 Lightnings in annual batches 'through the life of the project', likely to be at least another 25 years. In early 2017 the UK has 3 Lightnings in 17 Squadron, one in VMFAT-501 and a further 10 being delivered in batches of 4 and 6. Simple arithmetic shows that orders at this rate would reach the 138th aircraft in less than two decades. Little detail has been announced about when 809 NAS is to become operational and even less about plans to form further squadrons.

JOINT HELICOPTER COMMAND

Leonardo Helicopters MERLIN HC3, HC3i and planned HC4

Role Commando assault, load-lifting, troop movement
Engines 3 x Rolls Royce/Turbomeca RTM 322 each developing 2,100 shp
Length 74' 10" Rotor diameter 61' Height 21' 10"
Max Weight 32,120lb Max Speed 167 knots Crew 1 or 2 pilots, 1 aircrewman
Avionics Wescam MX-15 electro-optical/IR camera; defensive aids suite including directional IR countermeasures, AN/AAR-57 missile approach warning system, automatic chaff and flare dispensers
Armament 1 x M3M 0.5" machine-gun in cabin door; 1 x 7.62mm machine-gun in cabin window

Squadron Service 845, 846 Naval Air squadrons.

Notes
There are 7 aircraft modified to HC3i standard to allow a limited embarked capability as part of a TAG. They have power-folding main rotor heads, lashing points and improved communications. The basic HC3s, taken over from the RAF, lack these features and cannot be embarked. All 25 are to be upgraded to HC4 standard by Leonardo Helicopters at Yeovil with a 'glass cockpit' similar to that in the HM2, power-folding main rotor heads and tail pylons with other improvements but the last is not due to be delivered until 2022. 845 NAS has will eventually have 10 aircraft deployable in up to three TAG detachments and 846 NAS has an operational conversion/training flight, a maritime counter-terrorism flight and, eventually, a deployable TAG flight to back up 845. The remaining 5 airframes give some flexibility for the upgrade programme and act as attrition reserves.

Leonardo Helicopters WILDCAT AH1

Role Battlefield reconnaissance; airborne command and control, force protection and troop transport.
Engines 2 x LHTEC CTS 800-4N turboshafts each developing 1,362 shp
Length 50' Rotor diameter 42'   Height 12'
Max Weight 13,200lb   Max Speed 157 knots   Crew 2 pilots & 1 gunner
Avionics L-3 Wescam MX-15Di electro-optical/laser designator turret; digital mission planning system; Selex HIDAS 15 electronic warfare system
Armament Door-mounted 0.5 inch M3M machine gun.

Squadron Service 847 Naval Air Squadron, 1 Regiment Army Air Corps

Notes
847 NAS is shore-based at RNAS Yeovilton and operates the Wildcat AH 1 as part of the Commando Helicopter Force, within the Joint Helicopter Command, to support 3 Commando Brigade with battlefield reconnaissance and airborne command and control of forces on the ground. 1 Regiment is also based at RNAS Yeovilton and operates, effectively, as a joint force with the RN Wildcat squadrons. It comprises a headquarters squadron plus 652, 659 and 661 Squadrons which operate their Wildcats as a specialised intelligence, surveillance and reconnaissance aircraft in support of troops on the ground. In the troop-lift role, Army Wildcats can lift up to 5 fully-equipped troops over short distances. Like 847 NAS they can be embarked to form part of a TAG when required and AAC pilots are trained to operate from the sea.

Leonardo Helicopters APACHE AH1

Role Attack and armed reconnaissance helicopter
Engines 2 x Rolls Royce/Turbomeca RTM 322 turboshafts each developing 2,100 shp
Length 58' 3"   Rotor diameter 17' 2"   Height 15' 3"
Max Weight 15,075lb Max Speed 150 knots Crew 2 pilots
Avionics Selex HIDAS defensive aids suite; Longbow radar; optical and infrared target indication sensors.
Armament Up to 16 AGM-114 Hellfire air-to-surface guided weapons;
up to 4 Sidewinder air-to-air missiles; M230 30mm cannon with 1,160 rounds;
up to 76 CRV-7 unguided air-to-surface missiles.

Squadron Service 3 and 4 Regiments Army Air Corps

Notes
3 Regiment AAC comprises 653, 662 and 663 Squadrons. 4 Regiment comprises 656 and 664 Squadrons and both formations are based at the AAC base at Wattisham and form part of the Joint Helicopter Command. Apaches of 656 Squadron flew successfully on operations over Libya with a TAG embarked in OCEAN during 2011 and at least one unit is maintained at high readiness for embarked operations as part of a TAG but in an emergency a larger number of Apaches could be embarked if required.

Boeing CHINOOK HC4, HC4A and HC5

Role Battlefield transport helicopter
Engines 2 x Avco Lycoming T55-L-712 turboshafts each developing 3,750 shp
Length 98' 9"   Rotor diameter 60'   Height 18' 8"
Max weight 50,000lb Max speed 160 knots Crew 2 pilots & 2 aircrewmen/gunners
Avionics Infrared jammer; missile warning system; integrated digital 'glass cockpit';
moving map tablet and improved crewman's work station.
Armament up to 2 M 134 miniguns mounted in doorways; one M 60 machine gun on
rear loading ramp.

Squadron Service 7, 18, 27, 28(AC) Squadrons Royal Air Force

Notes
Operated by the RAF as part of the Joint Helicopter Force. Chinooks of 18 Squadron
embarked as part of a TAG in ARK ROYAL during the Second Gulf War in 2003. All four
squadrons are based at RAF Odiham in Hampshire from where the three operational
units could provide TAG detachments if required. The Chinook is too large to strike
down in OCEAN but QUEEN ELIZABETH's side lifts are sufficiently large to strike them
down fully spread and they could be embarked in significantly large numbers to support military or humanitarian operations. Chinooks can carry 54 fully-equipped
troops, 24 stretcher cases or loads of up to 44,000lb carried both internally and
externally over short distances. With extra fuel tanks they have a range of 1,000 nm
with a light load.

STEVE WRIGHT

BAE Systems HAWK T2

Role Advanced fast-jet training aircraft for RAF, RN and RM pilots
Engine 1 x Rolls Royce Adour 951 FADEC/turbofan delivering 6,500lb of thrust
Length 41'   **Wingspan** 32' 7"   **Height** 13' 1"
Max Weight 20,000lb   **Max Speed** Mach 1 at altitude   **Crew** 1 or 2 pilots
Avionics Two mission computers host simulations of sensor and weapons systems; a data link allows synthetic radar inputs for intercept training and synthetic electronic warfare threats. Inertial and GPS navigation systems.
Armament 7 hardpoints capable of carrying a total of 6,800lb of weapons, including 1 x 30mm cannon pod on centreline, AIM-9 Sidewinder or ASRAAM missiles and bombs.
Squadron Service 4(R) Squadron Royal Air Force

Notes
4 (Reserve) Squadron forms part of Number 4 Flying Training School at RAF Valley within the Military Flying Training System and provides advanced fast-jet training for RAF, RN and RM pilots up to the standard required for conversion onto operational types. The Hawk T 2 has a 'glass cockpit' with 3 full-colour, multi-function displays, similar to those in the Typhoon and F-35B, which display navigation, weapons and system information intended to immerse student pilots into a complex, data-rich tactical flying environment from the outset rather than just learning to fly the aircraft.

Short TUCANO T1

Role Basic fast-jet training aircraft for RAF, RN and RM pilots
Engine 1 x Garrett TPE 331-12B turboprop delivering 1,100 shp
Length 32' 4"   Wingspan 37'   Height 11' 2"
Max Weight 7,220lb   Max Speed 300 knots   Crew 1 or 2 pilots
Avionics Standard communications fit
Armament None
Squadron Service 72(R) Squadron Royal Air Force

Notes
Operated by 72 (Reserve) Squadron as part of Number 1 Flying Training School at RAF
Linton-on-Ouse, an element of the Military Flying Training System, the Tucano provides
basic training for student RAF, RN and RM fast-jet pilots and RAF weapons system operators; it handles like a jet aircraft but is significantly cheaper to operate. Ascent plans
to replace the Tucano with the Beechcraft T-6C Texan II in 2018.

Beech AVENGER T1

Role Observer training
Engines 2 x Pratt & Whitney PT6A-60A, each developing 1,050 shp
Length 46' 8" Wingspan 57' 11" Height 14' 4"
Max Weight 15,000lb Max Speed 313 knots
Crew 1 or 2 pilots, 4 student observers plus instructors
Avionics Surface search and ground mapping radar
Armament None

Squadron Service 750 Naval Air Squadron

Notes

Used by 750 NAS at RNAS Culdrose within the Military Flying Training System to provide Phase 3 training for RN observers and also lead in training for RAF AWACS systems operators. 'Phases 1 and 2 are carried out by 703 NAS at RAF Barkston Heath. The aircraft are civil-owned but military-registered.

LEE HOWARD

Grob TUTOR T1

Role Elementary training
Engine 1 x Textron Lycoming AE10-360-B1F developing 180 shp
Length 24' 9" Wingspan 32' 9" Height 7'
Max Weight 2,178lb Max Speed 185 knots Crew 2 pilots
Avionics None
Armament None

Squadron Service 703, 727 Naval Air Squadrons

Notes

'Tutors are used by 727 NAS within Navy Command for the flying grading of potential aircrew and other light tasks at RNAS Yeovilton and by 703 NAS within the Military Flying Training System at RAF Barkston Heath. In the latter unit they provide elementary flying training for student RN and RM helicopter pilots and lead-in, Phase 1 and 2 training, for RN observers.

Eurocopter SQUIRREL HT1

Role Basic helicopter training
Engine 1 x Turbomeca Ariel 2D developing 847 shp
Length 35' Rotor diameter 36' Height 9' 3"
Max Weight 5,225lb Max Speed 155 knots Crew 2 pilots plus up to 5 passengers
Avionics None
Armament None

Squadron Service 705 Naval Air Squadron

Notes

Used by 705 NAS within the Military Flying Training System as part of the Defence Helicopter Flying School at RAF Shawbury to teach basic helicopter handling, low flying, instrument flying and other skills to RN and RM pilots to prepare them for conversion to operational types. From 2018 Ascent is planning to replace them with Airbus H-135 twin-engined helicopters that are better suited to preparing pilots for the multi-engined types with full authority digital engine control and glass cockpits in front line service'.

LEE HOWARD

Eurocopter AS365N DAUPHIN 2

Role Passenger movement and training support
Engines 2 x Turbomeca Arriel 2C each developing 838 shp
Length 39' 9" Rotor diameter 39' 2" Height 13' 4"
Max Weight 9,480lb Max Speed 155 knots Crew 1 or 2 pilots plus up to 11 passengers
Avionics None
Armament None

Notes

Similar to the H-65 helicopters operated by the US Coast Guard, 2 of these civil-owned military-registered, COMR, helicopters are operated for the RN by Bond Helicopters under contract. They are maintained at Newquay airport and used to support FOST in the sea areas off Plymouth. They are commonly tasked to transfer passengers between ships at sea but can also undertake a wide variety of other roles. 'On a day-to-day basis they fly from an operating facility within Devonport Naval base from which FOST staff can be flown from their headquarters directly to ships at sea.

Royal Navy Historic Flight

Based at RNAS Yeovilton the Flight includes examples of the Fairey Swordfish, Hawker Sea Fury, Hawker Sea Hawk and de Havilland Chipmunk. They are flown by naval pilots and maintained by civilians under an MOD contract but not all are available at any one time.

Fly Navy Heritage Trust

The Trust owns the last airworthy Sea Vixen FAW 2, XP 924, which is operated alongside the RN Historic Flight and flown by naval pilots.

Sea Launched Missiles

Trident II D5

The American built Lockheed Martin Trident 2 (D5) submarine launched strategic missiles are Britain's only nuclear weapons and form the UK contribution to the NATO strategic deterrent. 16 missiles, each capable of carrying up to 6 UK manufactured thermonuclear warheads (but currently limited to 4 under current government policy), can be carried aboard each of the Vanguard class SSBNs. Trident has a maximum range of 12,000 km and is powered by a three stage rocket motor. Launch weight is 60 tonnes, overall length and width are 13.4 metres and 2.1 metres respectively.

Tomahawk (BGM-109)

This is a land attack cruise missile with a range of 1600 km and can be launched from a variety of platforms including surface ships and submarines. Some 65 of the latter version were purchased from America to arm Trafalgar class SSNs with the first being delivered to the Royal Navy for trials during 1998. Tomahawk is fired in a disposal container from the submarine's conventional torpedo tubes and is then accelerated to its subsonic cruising speed by a booster rocket motor before a lightweight F-107 turbojet takes over for the cruise. Its extremely accurate guidance system means that small targets can be hit with precision at maximum range, as was dramatically illustrated in the Gulf War and Afghanistan. Total weight of the submarine version, including its launch capsule is 1816 kg, it carries a 450 kg warhead, length is 6.4 metres and wingspan (fully extended) 2.54 m. Fitted in Astute & T class submarines. It was announced in 2014 that the US Navy are to stop procuring the missile in 2015 which has implications for the production line, although an MoD spokesman expected this not to impact on UK requirements.

Harpoon

The Harpoon is a sophisticated anti-ship missile using a combination of inertial guidance and active radar homing to attack targets out to a range of 130 km, cruising at Mach 0.9 and carrying a 227 kg warhead. It is powered by a lightweight turbojet but is accelerated at launch by a booster rocket. Fitted to Type 23 frigates and four Type 45 destroyers. Harpoon is planned to be retired from Royal Navy service at the end of 2018, without replacement.

Sea Viper (Aster 15/30)

Two versions of the Aster missile equip the Type 45 Destroyer, the shorter range Aster 15 and the longer range Aster 30. The missiles form the weapon component of the Principal Anti Air Missile System (PAAMS). Housed in a 48 cell Sylver Vertical Launch system, the missile mix can be loaded to match the ships requirement. Aster 15 has a range of 30 km while Aster 30 can achieve 100 km. The prime external difference between the two is the size of the booster rocket attached to the bottom of the missile. PAAMS is known as Sea Viper in RN service.

Sea Wolf

Short range rapid reaction anti-missile missile and anti-aircraft weapon. The complete weapon system, including radars and fire control computers, is entirely automatic in operation. Type 23 frigates carry 32 Vertical Launch Seawolf (VLS) in a silo on the foredeck. Basic missile data: weight 82 kg, length 1.9 m, wingspan 56 cm, range c.5-6 km, warhead 13.4 kg. The VLS missile is basically similar but has jettisonable tandem boost rocket motors.

Sea Ceptor

Incorporating the Common Anti-Air Modular Missile (CAAMM) family, being developed to replace the Rapier and Seawolf SAM systems, plus the ASRAAM short range Air-to-Air Missile. It will arm the Royal Navy's Type 23 frigates and its Type 26 Global Combat Ships. In Spring 2012 the MoD awarded MBDA UK a five-year Demonstration Phase contract worth £483 million to develop the missile for the RN. In September 2013 a £250 million contract was announced to manufacture the missile in the UK, sustaining around 250 jobs at MBDA sites in Stevenage, Filton and Lostock. Installation of the Sea Ceptor on Type 23 frigates started in 2015 with ARGYLL and the last will be completed by 2021. CAMM missiles will be fitted in the existing VL Seawolf silo (one canister per cell for a maximum of 32 missiles).

Guns

114mm Vickers Mk8 Mod 1

The Royal Navy's standard medium calibre general purpose gun which arms the Type 23 frigates and Type 45 destroyers. The Mod 1 is an electrically operated version of the original gun and is recognised by its angular turret. First introduced in 2001 it is now fitted in all Type 23 and Type 45 vessels. Rate of fire: 25 rounds/min. Range: 22,000 m. Weight of Shell: 21 kg.

Goalkeeper

A highly effective automatic Close in Weapons System (CIWS) designed to shoot down missiles and aircraft which have evaded the outer layers of a ships defences. The complete system, designed and built in Holland, is on an autonomous mounting and includes radars, fire control computers and a 7-barrel 30 mm Gatling gun firing 4200 rounds/min. Goalkeeper is designed to engage targets between 350 and 1500 metres away. However, with the decommissioning of the BIII Type 22 frigates and the carrier ILLUSTRIOUS there remains just the two mounts on BULWARK. These will be removed when she enters refit in 2017.

Phalanx

A US built CIWS designed around the Vulcan 20 mm rotary cannon. Rate of fire is 3000 rounds/min and effective range is c.1500 m. Fitted in Type 45, OCEAN and some Wave, Bay and Fort classes. Block 1B began entering service from 2009. Incorporates side mounted Forward looking infra-red enabling CIWS to engage low aircraft and surface craft. In October 2012 it was announced that a further five Phalanx Block 1B mountings were to be procured to protect RFA ships.

DS30B 30mm

Single mounting carrying an Oerlikon 30mm gun. Fitted to Type 23 frigates and various patrol vessels and MCMVs. In August 2005 it was announced that the DS30B fitted in Type 23 frigates was to be upgraded to DS30M Mk 2 to include new direct-drive digital servos and the replacement of the earlier Oerlikon KCB cannon with the ATK Mk 44 Bushmaster II 30 mm gun. Consideration is already being given to purchasing additional DS30M Mk 2 systems for minor war vessels and auxiliaries.

GAM BO 20mm

A simple hand operated mounting carrying a single Oerlikon KAA 200 automatic cannon firing 1000 rounds/min. Maximum range is 2000 m. Carried by most of the fleet's major warships except the Type 23 frigates.

20mm Mk.7A

The design of this simple but reliable weapon dates back to World War II but it still provides a useful increase in firepower, particularly for auxiliary vessels and RFAs. Rate of fire 500-800 rounds/min.

Close Range Weapons

In addition to the major weapons systems, all RN ships carry a variety of smaller calibre weapons to provide protection against emerging terrorist threats in port and on the high seas such as small fast suicide craft. In addition it is sometimes preferable, during policing or stop and search operations to have a smaller calibre weapon available. Depending upon the operational environment ships may be seen armed with varying numbers of pedestal mounted General Purpose Machine Guns (GPMG). Another addition to the close in weapons is the Mk 44 Mini Gun a total of 150 of which have been procured from the United States as a fleetwide fit. Fitted to a naval post mount, the Minigun is able to fire up to 3,000 rounds per minute, and is fully self-contained (operating off battery power).

Torpedoes

Sting Ray

A lightweight anti-submarine torpedo which can be launched from ships, helicopters or aircraft. In effect it is an undersea guided missile with a range of 11 km at 45 knots or 7.5 km at 60 knots. Length 2.1 m, diameter 330 mm. Type 23s have the Magazine Torpedo Launch System (MTLS) with internal launch tubes. Sting Ray Mod 1 is intended to prosecute the same threats as the original Sting Ray but with an enhanced capability against small conventionally powered submarines and an improved shallow-water performance.

Spearfish

Spearfish is a submarine-launched heavyweight torpedo which has replaced Tigerfish. Claimed by the manufacturers to be the world's fastest torpedo, capable of over 70 kts, its sophisticated guidance system includes an onboard acoustic processing suite and tactical computer backed up by a command and control wire link to the parent submarine. Over 20ft in length and weighing nearly two tons, Spearfish is fired from the standard 21-inch submarine torpedo tube and utilises an advanced bi-propellant gas turbine engine for higher performance. To undergo a £270 million upgrade which will include a new warhead, a change to the fuel system to improve safety, full digitisation of the weapon and a new fibre optic guidance link to improve performance. The work is to be carried out by BAE Systems at Portsmouth with deliveries beginning in 2020 and continuing to 2024.

Future Weapons

Sea Venom

Formerly known as the Future Anti-Surface Guided Weapon (Heavy), Sea Venom is high-subsonic 'drop-launch' missile in the 110 kg-class incorporating an imaging infrared seeker (with provisions for an additional semi-active laser guidance channel), a two-way datalink for operator-in-the-loop control, and a 30kg warhead. Designed by MBDA to replace the helicopter air-launched Exocet, the missile will have a range of up to 25 km and will be able to counter targets up to corvette size. The FASGW programme, comprising both Heavy and Light missiles, is a joint venture between the UK and France. The missile will equip the RNs Wildcat helicopter and, in July 2014, AgustaWestland received a £90 million contract to integrate the respective variants for deployment from the Wildcat HMA2. Each aircraft will be able to carry four missiles and it is anticipated that Initial Operating Capability will be achieved in 2020, although there are aspirations that this date will move left.

Martlet

Formerly known as the Future Anti-Surface Guided Weapon (Light), this missile is designed to counter small boat and fast inshore attack craft threats. It is based on the laser beam-riding variant of the Thales Lightweight Multi-role Missile (LMM). With a range of up to 8 km it carries a 3 kg blast fragmentation/shaped charge warhead travelling at about Mach 1.5. Missiles will be carried in a five-round launcher (with each Wildcat able to carry up to four launchers). Alternatively a mix of two Sea Venom on the outer pylon and two five round Martlet on the inner weapons station can be carried. An active laser guidance unit integrated within the L-3 Wescam nose turret will support laser beam-riding guidance. Trials of both variants of FASGW are planned to take place between late 2018 to late 2019.

At the end of the line ...

Readers may well find other warships afloat which are not mentioned in this book. The majority have fulfilled a long and useful life and are now relegated to non-seagoing duties. The following list gives details of their current duties:

Pennant No	Ship	Remarks
D23	BRISTOL	Type 82 Destroyer - Sea Cadet Training Ship at Portsmouth.
M29	BRECON	Hunt Class Minehunter - Attached to the New Entry Training Establishment, HMS RALEIGH, Torpoint, as a static Seamanship Training Ship.
M103	CROMER	Single Role Minehunter - Attached to BRNC, Dartmouth as a Static Training Ship.
L3505	SIR TRISTRAM	Refitted as a Static Range Vessel at Portland.
S50	COURAGEOUS	Nuclear-powered Submarine - On display at Devonport Naval Base. Can be visited during Base Tours. Tel: 01752 552326 for details.
C35	BELFAST	World War II Cruiser Museum ship - Pool of London. Open to the public daily. Tel: 020 7940 6300
D73 S17	CAVALIER OCELOT	World War II Destroyer & Oberon class Submarine Museum Ships at Chatham. Open to the public. Tel: 01634 823800
S67	ALLIANCE	Submarine - Museum Ship at Gosport Open to the public daily. Tel: 023 92 511349
LCT7074	LANDFALL	A D-Day veteran. Refloated in October 2014 six years after she sank at Birkenhead. Undergoing restoration by the NMRN at Portsmouth. Eventually to be displayed outside the D-Day Museum, Southsea.
M1115	BRONINGTON	Sank at Birkenhead, its future now uncertain.
	BRITANNIA	Ex Royal Yacht at Leith. Open to the public.
	CAROLINE	Light Cruiser and veteran of the Battle of Jutland preserved at Belfast. Closed for hull conservation. Re-opening February 2017.
	M33	Coastal Monitor and veteran of the Gallipoli Campaign on display at Portsmouth as part of the National Museum of the Royal Navy.

The Leaf class support tanker RFA ORANGELEAF leaving Birkenhead under tow of tug DIAVLOS PRIDE on 24 February 2016 bound for recycling in Turkey.

At the time of publishing (December 2016) the following ships were laid up in long term storage or awaiting sale.

PORTSMOUTH: Walney.

PLYMOUTH: Tireless; Trafalgar; Turbulent; Sceptre; Superb; Splendid; Spartan; Sovereign; Conqueror; Valiant; Warspite.

ROSYTH: Resolution; Renown; Repulse; Revenge; Swiftsure; Churchill; Dreadnought.

BIRKENHEAD: Black Rover, Diligence.

Since the previous edition the following vessels in long term storage or awaiting scrap were disposed of:

ORANGELEAF: Departed Birkenhead under tow of tug DIAVLOS PRIDE on 24 February 2016 bound for recycling at Leyal Shipbreakers, Turkey.

ENDURANCE: Departed Portsmouth under tow of tug SPARTAN on 1 June 2016 bound for recycling at Leyal Shipbreakers, Turkey.

ILLUSTRIOUS: Sold for recycling at Leyal Shipbreakers, Turkey. Was scheduled to depart Portsmouth in late October/early November 2016 but at time of going to press (25 November) remained at Portsmouth.